Published in the United States by Nyansa Classical Community
2416 S. Derbigny St.
New Orleans, LA 70125
nyansaclassicalcommunity.org

To order additional materials, please go to www.nyansaclassicalcommunity.org

ISBN: 978-1-967443-00-0 (paperback)
ISBN: 978-1-967443-01-7 (eBook)

Cover design by Laura Duffy
Book design by Sarah Scudder
Greek Myth poetry written by Ahnia Leary
Illustrations by Josslyn Littles and Eve Singer
Content developed by Dr. Angel Adams Parham and Interns of Nyansa Classical Community

Printed in the United States of America

Credits

All literature images created by Josslyn Littles and Eve Singer

Greek Myth poetry written by Ahnia Leary

Formatting and Design by Sarah Scudder

Acknowledgement

Thank you to the following organization for their support and funding:

Nyansa Classical Community

Founded by Dr. Angel Adams Parham, Nyansa Classical Community provides classical, Christian curricula and programming designed to connect with and draw students from diverse backgrounds into the beauty of classical literature and the Great Conversation. For more information, please go to nyansaclassicalcommunity.org.

Nyansa Materials

This workbook is intended to be used alongside our Year One Elementary Curricula. This book should be purchased with Nyansa Teacher's Guide and Year One Elementary Literature Workbook.

To order additional materials please go to:
www.nyansaclassicalcommunity.org

Literature Group Week 1– Demeter
Day 1
Lesson 1: Demeter - Greek Goddess of the Earth

Focus Virtue: Love is caring for a person or thing very much and wishing good towards them.

Focus Vice: Hate is disliking a person or thing very much and wishing harm towards them.

Today, we will be discussing love and hate. Discuss what each means. Create a new memory card for each term with its meaning and its opposite on the back of the card. These can be used for memory-matching games once there are enough of them. Identify themes that go with the story and write terms and definitions on flash cards. Flash cards are also available for purchase through our website.

READ:

Read the story of Demeter and Persephone (Greek Gods #1). Encourage narration activities as students listen (drawing, writing, etc). During a narration activity, the instructor reads a story, and afterward, the children tell the story back. The process helps them to deepen their listening, comprehension, and presentation skills. This telling or narrating back can be done verbally, with drawings, acting the story out, etc. Each student should have a narration notebook that can be used for drawing and writing.

For more examples, see our Teacher's Guide.
Use the following illustrations for this week.

DEMETER AND PERSEPHONE

One of the Greeks' favorite goddesses was Demeter, the goddess of the earth and of the harvest. In our own day, you may have heard people use the term "Mother Earth," and the Greeks thought of Demeter in that way - she was a kind, motherly person, and the Greeks prayed to her in hopes of getting a good harvest out of the ground. Demeter was also one of Zeus' sisters and, therefore, one of the more important and powerful goddesses. The Greeks believed that Demeter caused crops to grow, trees to bud, and flowers to blossom. They particularly loved to draw Demeter on vases. In these drawings, she often wears a crown and has sheaves of wheat or flowers in her hands. This story gives the Greeks an explanation for why plants only grow for three-quarters of the year - because of Demeter's love for her daughter Persephone.

Hades, the grim god of the dead, wanted a wife, but no one wanted to live with him in Erebos, his dark and cold land. So Hades asked Zeus for a wife, and Zeus promised him the hand of beautiful Persephone, Demeter's graceful daughter. Persephone loved flowers more than anything else, and she delighted to dance in the sun next to her kind mother. Zeus knew that Persephone would never go with Hades willingly, so he tricked the young woman into leaving her mother's side by creating a most marvelous flower in a meadow far away. Persephone was delighted by the gorgeous flower, but when she reached down to pick it, the ground opened up, and Hades emerged with a chariot and four black horses! Hades picked up Persephone, dropped her into his chariot, and plunged back into the earth. With a scream from Persephone, the ground closed back up behind them, leaving no trace of Demeter's sun-loving daughter.

Before long, Demeter realized Persephone was missing. Demeter loved her daughter more than anything else, and for nine days, she walked all over the earth looking for her beloved child. In all that time, she did not eat, drink, or bathe. Eventually, the other gods took pity on her, and Helios, the sun god, confessed that he had seen Hades steal her daughter. Thinking of her beautiful sun-loving daughter as a prisoner in that cold and dreary world with stern Hades made Demeter weep. She was so sad that she sat huddled in a heap and could not be comforted. When she realized Zeus was behind it all, she refused to set foot on Mount Olympus again until she had her daughter back. She also refused to allow another seed to sprout from the ground until Hades returned Persephone.

Up on his lofty throne, shining Zeus realized the situation was getting desperate. If no crops grew upon the earth, all the people would die, and there would be no one to worship the gods! So he sent the messenger god, Hermes, down to dark Erebos to bring back Persephone.

"But," warned Zeus sternly, "if she has eaten any food from the underworld, she will have to remain there." Hermes sped away to Erebos on his winged sandals.

Before the dark throne, Hermes said, "Oh lord Hades, god of death and spirits, Zeus orders you to return the lovely Persephone, for if you fail, Demeter will cause no seed to grow out of the ground, and all of mankind will die."

Hades reluctantly agreed, but he pulled Persephone aside to talk with her first. He said, "Oh my lovely bride, please do not think harshly of me, for I would have been a good and gentle husband to you and made you my queen of all the underworld. And now, take as a small gift from me, a pomegranate seed to eat on your journey back to the land of the living."

And with that, he kissed her and returned her to Hermes. Persephone smiled a gentle smile - she was so happy to return to her loving mother, and yet Hades had surprised her with his gentleness and kindness. She happily ate the seed and skipped behind Hermes all the way back to the sunlit land above.

Up to Demeter's fair temple, they sped. When Demeter saw Persephone, her heart leaped. Demeter ran to Persephone and wrapped her in her arms. Suddenly, she felt afraid; what if something had gone wrong?

"My dearest daughter," said Demeter all of a sudden, "Did you eat anything down in the underworld? Please tell me at once!"

"Not at first, Mother, but Hades gave me a pomegranate seed as I was leaving, and I ate it. Was that wrong?" Persephone looked anxiously up at her mother.

Demeter clung to her daughter, unwilling to give her back. But wise Zeus proposed a compromise: Persephone would spend three months every year with Hades, but the rest of the year she could live on the good green earth with her mother if Demeter agreed to make the crops grow again. Joyfully, both of them agreed. Demeter ran over the whole earth, Persephone at her side. As they ran, crops sprouted, trees budded, and flowers pushed through the tender soil all over the earth. And so, the Greeks believed that winter came because Demeter sat and mourned for her daughter for three months every year, but when Persephone returned, spring came again, and life grew everywhere upon the earth because of Demeter's love and joy.

Cultural Note: Sometimes, the Greeks drew Demeter carrying a cornucopia. The word "cornucopia" means "horn of plenty." You may have seen a picture of one around Thanksgiving time - it looks like a horn-shaped basket full of crops like pumpkins, apples, wheat, and so on. Even today, although Americans do not worship Demeter, we use a cornucopia to represent a harvest celebration.

- *After narration activities are completed, have children practice saying the memory sentence for the Demeter story.*
- *Discuss children's responses to the discussion questions provided with the story, and/ or create your own discussion questions.*
- *Copywork, poetry, brainstorming, and dictation activity worksheets are available in our Year One Literature Workbook. See our website for more information.*

DISCUSS:

Discussion Questions:

1. Who demonstrated love in this story? Do you see any hate in the story?
2. Why did Hades give Persephone the pomegranate seed to eat? Was that a loving thing to do?
3. Why did Zeus agree to give Persephone back to Demeter? Do you think the compromise was fair?
4. Have you ever lost someone or something you loved very much?

MEMORY:

Memory Sentence: Demeter loved Persephone and got her back from Hades.

FOLLOW-UP ACTIVITIES:

1. **DRESS UP**

   - Have the children act out the story. Keeping a dress-up box with items that go with the story allows the children to act the story out with relevant props. Here are some suggested dress-up items for the Demeter story:

   - Suggested dress-up items:

flowers	blue robe (Demeter)
basket of produce	crown (Demeter)
pomegranate seed	sandals (Hermes)
black robe (Hades)	tiara (Persephone)

2. **BRAINSTORM**

   - Print out the full-page image of Demeter. All Greek Myth illustrations can be purchased separately through our website. Tape or glue this image to a large piece of planning paper. You will work with the children to brainstorm descriptive words that go along with the story of Demeter. These words will become a word bank for the children to write poetry, narrative summaries, etc. When writing poetry, the haiku poetry form is ideal as it is simple and allows for reinforcing the idea of syllables for young children.

   - Below are some words that work for the main characters and places mentioned in the story. Feel free to let the kids come up with their own words, but if they're having trouble, you can get things going by suggesting some on the lists below. Write the main persons, places, and things from the story up on a whiteboard or paper with space beneath them. Brainstorm descriptive words to go under each OR have descriptive words written in advance on stickies for younger kids. In the case of younger children, call out each term and ask for a student volunteer to put each term under the person, place, or thing that it describes. Keep this for the next session.

People

- Demeter - goddess of the earth, kind, loving, mature, maternal, motherly, tender, affectionate, sad, protective, heartbroken

- Persephone - sun-loving, young, sweet, beautiful, stolen, sad, graceful

- Hades - stern, dark, cold, selfish, thief, trickster

- Zeus - lofty, king of the gods, promise-maker, regretful, worried

- Hermes - messenger, quick, speedy

- Helios - god of the sun, compassionate, truthful

Places

- Earth - beautiful, sunny, grassy, covered with flowers, delightful, full of life

- Erebos - dark, gloomy, cold, land of the dead

- When you finish this brainstorming, be sure to keep the large planning paper with all of the different words on it. This should be posted on the wall if possible so it can be a continued point of reference. This will be useful in helping children to remember the story and will act as the word bank for their poetry.

- Use the Nyansa Year One Literature Workbook and have students record the brainstorming words in the "brainstorming" section.

For more examples, see our Teacher's Guide.

Literature Group Week 1– Demeter
Day 2

Focus Virtue: Love is caring for a person or thing very much and wishing good towards them.

Focus Vice: Hate is disliking a person or thing very much and wishing harm towards them.

DISCUSS:

- Review the concepts "love" and "hate". Use the memory cards created for the previous session.
- Review the memory sentences presented in the previous session.

FOLLOW-UP ACTIVITIES:

1. DICTATION:

- Individual

  Introduce the dictation activity. Dictation is an activity that helps students to strengthen their skills of listening, writing, and spelling. For children who are able to write, the activity consists in the instructor slowly reading the dictation text as the students attempt to write exactly what is being said, including punctuation.

  We divide the dictation sentences into three increasing levels of difficulty: pre-k and kindergarten; early elementary; and later elementary. For pre-K and kindergarten, rather than writing out a sentence, children are given a dictation sheet which simply has a choice of letters for four items. The instructor reads the word and students circle or underline the letter choice which shows the sound the word starts with. See the dictation worksheet in the Appendix for pre-k and kindergarten.

  For children who can write and spell, repeat the sentence or sentences a few times, speaking slowly and clearly to give them plenty of time to get it down as accurately as possible.

  Students can record their dictation in the "dictation" section of the Year One Elementary Literature Workbook.

- Dictation as a Team

  To make this into a game, divide the children into teams. They will do their dictation exercise separately at first, but each person on the team who gets the dictation correct will get two points. Team members who make mistakes will get one point for their efforts.

  Before the instructor writes the correct sentence on the board, consider allowing team members to review each other's work and discuss corrections. This way, the children can help each other, and each team maximizes their number of points.

Pre-K

The Pre-K exercises are provided on a worksheet in a separate document, Year One Dictation Sheets, for purchase.

- Demeter - begins with N, D, A, or P
- Winter - begins with N, O, W, or K
- Hades- begins with H, R, Q, or T
- Sun- begins with U, K, S, or E

Early Elementary

(Directions: Say the sentence one time. Have your students repeat the sentence after you. Have the students write down as much of the sentence as they can remember. Then, say the sentence again at the end and have your student check to see if they wrote the sentence correctly. You might need to write up uncommon names on a board for students to copy. For more information and examples, see Teacher's Guide). You can also use the Year One Literature Workbook to record the dictation sentences.

- Demeter was sad that Hades took her girl.
- Demeter was sad that Hades stole Persephone to be his wife.

Later Elementary

- Demeter was so sad to lose Persephone that she stopped helping the crops to grow.
- Zeus made Hades give Persephone back to Demeter for most of the year.

Note: Dictation is an important exercise to build a habit of attention and reinforce writing skills. For the Pre-K, see our website for Year One Dictation Sheets.

2. CREATIVE WRITING:

- Once dictation is done, if there's still time left, go back to the brainstorming page with the word bank and complete if there's still more to be done. If it was completed last session, then introduce the haiku form and show them the sample haiku based on some of the words from the brainstorming exercise. Here's an example from words provided in this guide:

> *Demeter is sad (5 syllables)*
> *Hades, dark, selfish trickster (7 syllables)*
> *Steals Persephone *(5 syllables)*

*Persephone is pronounced [pur-se-fa-nee])

- Each child's poetry should be written into their individual narration notebook. You can also use Nyansa's Year One Elementary Literature Workbook. If the child is too young to write, they can dictate to an adult who writes for them. Compile these poems into a single program notebook, carefully labeling each poem with the correct child's name. At the end of the year, these can be bound into a poetry book and duplicated so that each family has a copy. This end-of-year publication may also include children's artwork, narrative summaries, reflections, etc. It's a wonderful memory book and provides lots of pride for both children and parents to see what their children have produced. This book will also act as a gathering of memories that help students to remember all that they have learned about this year.

See Teacher's Guide for more examples.

3. CLOSING GAME SUGGESTIONS:

- Number Knockout - links and explanations of this game can be found in our Teacher's Guide book, available for purchase on our website.

- Review games - these include Latin and other review games for our literature curriculum. For example, use 3x5 cards. Put the names of the gods and goddesses on one side of the card and what they are known for on a separate 3x5 card. Throughout the weeks, you can review the gods and goddesses by matching the name of the god or goddess with what they are known for. For more ideas, see our Teacher's Guide.

Literature Group Week 1– Demeter
Day 3

REVIEW: Review the concepts of love and hate. Use the memory cards created for the previous session. Ask the students to recall the memory sentence for this story.

MEMORIZE:

Introduce the poem below, which students can memorize as a way of remembering the key aspects of the story. The text can be recited as poetry, or it can be rapped or sung if the students would like to add melody or beats.

The Goddess Demeter

A beautiful goddess of Heaven and rebirth,
Demeter was known to be a mother to the Earth,
Flowers bloomed from her beauty and love,
She was a powerful goddess in the sky above.
Her daughter Persephone loved nature and the sun,
Through the meadows and fields, she was delighted to run.
Until one day Hades wanted a wife,
He begged Zeus to give him part of her life.
Persephone was doomed to the underworld,
Demeter had lost her lovely little girl.
She cried and cried for three months straight.
Because Persephone was doomed to a gloomy fate.
From Hades Pomegranate were three berries she ate.
And now winter lasts three full months long,
When Demeter cries, not a smile nor song.
The other nine months are filled with cheer,
Because spring, summer, and Persephone are here!

.

FOLLOW-UP ACTIVITIES:

1. CREATIVE WRITING:

- Work with the children on their own original poetry based on the story of Demeter. Use the word bank created earlier in the week.

- Have older children work on writing their own version of the Demeter story with illustrations. This is best done in their individual notebook, lined on one side and blank on the other. See the Appendix for photos of this kind of notebook with sample student writing and illustrations. Or, record the student's poem in Nyansa's Year One Literature Workbook.

- Close out the story of Demeter by inviting students to present the poetry, pictures, and/or other writing they have done this week.

2. CLOSING GAME SUGGESTIONS:

- Number Knockout - links and explanations of this game can be found in our Teacher's Guide book, available for purchase on our website.

- Review games - these include Latin and other review games for our literature curriculum. For example, use 3x5 cards. Put the names of the gods and goddesses on one side of the card and what they are known for on a separate 3x5 card. Throughout the weeks, you can review the gods and goddesses by matching the name of the god or goddess with what they are known for. For more ideas, see our Teacher's Guide.

Literature Group Week 1– Demeter Day 4

See Learning Through Art

On day four, we encourage you to use the Nyansa Art Curriculum. Students will learn to build observation skills and habits of attention. They will also engage in group discussions that discuss our virtues for the week.

If you do not have the Nyansa Year One Art Curriculum, you can use the illustrations from this week's lessons. Have your students look at the illustration for 2 minutes. After the two minutes, turn over the page. Ask your student to describe the illustration back to you without looking at the picture. Then, discuss how the illustrations for this week tell the story of this week's Greek Myth through the images they observed.

Literature Group Week 2– Aphrodite
Day 1
Lesson 1: Aphrodite - Greek Goddess of Love

Focus Virtue: Compassion is feeling sorry for those who are suffering and wanting to help.

Focus Vice: Indifference is ignoring the suffering or needs of others.

Today we will be discussing compassion and indifference.. Discuss what each means. Create a new memory card for each term with its meaning and its opposite on the back of the card. These can be used for memory-matching games once there are enough of them. Identify themes that go with the story and write terms and definitions on flash cards. Introduce the story of Aphrodite by allowing the students two minutes to examine her portrait. Then, turn over the portrait and ask the students to recall what they saw. Use the portrait discussion and the following facts to introduce the story:

Introduction:

In ancient Greece, Aphrodite was the goddess of love and beauty. Aphrodite loved graceful and gentle things, and they often painted her with swans, doves, and swallows. Legends about Aphrodite's family disagree. Some say that Aphrodite was born in the sea and that she rose out of the foamy waves, but other legends say she was one of Zeus' many daughters. Either way, the Greeks thought of her as coming to them from the sea, almost like a mermaid. They also considered sweet-smelling roses, pink apples, and graceful myrtle leaves as sacred to the gentle goddess. For people in love, Aphrodite was a goddess of compassionate help and encouragement, as you will see in the story of Atalanta.

Use the following illustrations for this week.

Read the story of Aphrodite and Atalanta (Greek Gods #2). Encourage narration activities as students listen (drawing, writing, etc).

Aphrodite and Atalanta

When Atalanta was born, her father, the king of Arkadia, ordered his servants to throw her into the woods because she wasn't a boy. The gods, however, sent a mother bear to nurse the sweet baby. Little Atalanta grew up racing the deer through the forest. By the time Atalanta was a young woman, she was an incredibly fast runner and a brave hero. She became so famous that her father found her again and invited her to come home.

Atalanta accepted her father's invitation, but as soon as she did, her father announced that she should marry a local prince. Swift Atalanta had no intention of getting married. None of the princes interested her, but she knew if she simply refused to marry all of the princes, she might offend them and cause trouble. So clever Atalanta proposed the following plan: she would run a race against any prince who wanted to marry her. If the prince won, she would marry him. If she won, the prince would die!

Several of the local princes were eager to run a race against the beautiful princess, but Atalanta beat them without even trying, and each prince was put to death. Atalanta was pleased - she would remain single after all! But sweet Aphrodite was not happy. She felt compassion for all the brave young men who were dying trying to marry Atalanta. She resolved to watch over Atalanta and find an opportunity to make the young woman find love.

Months passed, and a new prince came to town, Prince Melanion. He heard cheering on the main street, and as he walked over to see what was going on - WOOSH! Atalanta ran by, her hair streaming in the wind. She moved so gracefully that her feet did not even bend the blades of grass. And just like that, Melanion fell in love with Atalanta. His heart filled with longing and despair. He had heard all about the racing. No one could beat a runner like Atalanta. Tears filled his eyes.

Aphrodite saw his tears and resolved that no more men would die for the love of Atalanta. All at once, Aphrodite appeared to him. Melanion was startled to see the goddess. She seemed like a tall, graceful woman with large, gentle eyes and a flowing blue dress. In her long hair were flowers, and she wore a wreath of myrtle on her head.

"Do you love Atalanta, my sad young prince?" she asked.

"Oh, I do!" replied Melanion, "but I am not so foolish as to believe I could beat her. She is as swift as the wind. I would surely die trying to win her."

"Leave that to me," said Aphrodite, "I will give you three of my very own golden apples. Carry them with you when you race Atalanta. As you run, throw the apples one by one away from the racecourse as far as you can. Do as I say, and you will marry your love!"

"Sweet Aphrodite, thank you!" said the prince, and he kissed the hem of her dress.

Encouraged by Aphrodite's kindness, the prince went to the palace to begin a race with the swift princess. Looking at the handsome young man before him, the king urged him to reconsider.

But Melanion smiled a modest smile and said, "Oh king, your daughter is the strongest and fastest and most courageous woman a man could ever hope to marry. If I cannot marry her, I will gladly die." Impressed, the king agreed to let Melanion race Atalanta the very next day.

All the people of Arkadia gathered along the racetrack to watch the contest. Melanion was the most impressive prince to run against their princess yet. As Atalanta watched him tie his sandals before the race, she felt sad that such a handsome and noble prince would die. Aphrodite saw the first glimmer of compassion in the girl's heart and rejoiced!

The race was off! With the joy of a prancing deer, Atalanta sped down the track as always, but then something new happened. She looked behind her at the courageous prince. He was far behind her and seemed to be struggling with one of his pockets. Surprised, she saw him throw a golden ball to the side of the track. Burning curiosity seized her, and she turned aside to find the shiny ball. When she reached it, she saw that it was a golden apple. The sweet goddess Aphrodite had enchanted the apple. To Melanion, it had seemed as light as feathers, but to Atalanta, it was as heavy as lead. But Atalanta kept it anyway.

Running a little slower with the apple, Atalanta overtook Melanion again, but just as she did, he threw his second golden apple, even farther this time into the woods. Her heart filled with longing for the pretty fruit, and so again she ran to get it. This apple was even heavier, and she struggled to catch up with him. He threw his third apple, and again, she ran after it. She struggled to carry all three in her arms as she ran.

Looking up, she saw Melanion closing in on the finish line. She ran with all her might, but he passed the finish line just ahead of her. Atalanta looked up into his kind face, and her heart leaped with joy. She would happily marry him. Aphrodite appeared next to the couple, looking like a village maiden with baskets of roses. Smiling, she threw the petals on the happy couple and winked secretly at Melanion. Love had triumphed!

Language Note: Aphrodite gets her name from the Greek word, "aphros" which means foam!

- *After narration activities are completed, have children practice saying the memory sentence for the story.*
- *Discuss children's responses to the discussion questions provided with the story, and/or create your own discussion questions.*
- *Copywork, poetry, brainstorming, and dictation activity worksheets are available in our Year One Elementary Literature Workbook. See our website for more information.*

DISCUSS:

Discussion Questions:

1. How did Aphrodite have compassion on Melanion?

2. Why do you think Atalanta didn't want to ever get married? Is it fair that Aphrodite interceded in her life and helped Melanion?

3. Why was Atalanta indifferent to the men who wanted to marry her? What was the consequence of her indifference?

4. Why did Atalanta look behind her at Melanion? Why did she stop to get the apples?

5. Have you ever seen someone sad or in pain and stopped to help? How did it feel to make another person feel better?

6. Many people say that the opposite of love is not hate but indifference. What are your thoughts on this? Why might people believe that?

MEMORY:

Memory Sentence: Compassionate Aphrodite helped Melanion beat swift Atalanta in a race.

FOLLOW-UP ACTIVITIES:

1. **DRESS UP**

    - Have the children act out the story. Keeping a dress-up box with items that go with the story allows the children to act the story out with relevant props. Suggested dress-up items:

sandals	gold painted apples
wreath of leaves (Aphrodite)	crown
blue scarf/robe (Aphrodite)	

2. BRAINSTORM

- Print out the full-page image of Aphrodite, which is in the Appendix. Tape or glue this image to a large piece of planning paper. You will work with the children to brainstorm descriptive words that go along with the story of Aphrodite. These words will become a word bank that the children will use to write poetry, narrative summaries, etc. When writing poetry, the haiku poetry form is ideal as it is simple and allows for reinforcing the idea of syllables for young children.

- Here below are some words that work for the main characters and places mentioned in the story. Feel free to let the kids come up with their own words, but if they're having trouble, you can get things going by suggesting some on the lists below. Write the main persons, places, and things from the story up on a whiteboard or paper with space beneath them. Brainstorm descriptive words to go under each OR have descriptive words written in advance on stickies for younger kids. In the case of younger children, call out each term and ask for a student volunteer to put each term under the person, place, or thing that it describes. Keep this for the next session.

People

- Aphrodite - goddess of love, beautiful, kind, compassionate, lovely
- Atalanta - brave, fast, beautiful, indifferent, independant, swift, clever, princess, famous
- Melanion - brave, handsome, strong, courageous, prince, dejected, encouraged
- King of Arkadia - selfish, cruel, father, curious

Things

- Golden apples - glowing, beautiful, changing, precious, heavy

---

- When you finish this brainstorming, be sure to keep the large planning paper with all of the different words on it. This should be posted on the wall if possible so it can be a continued point of reference. This will be useful in helping children to remember the story and will act as the word bank for their poetry.

- Use the Nyansa Year One Literature Workbook and have students record the brainstorming words in the "brainstorming" section.

For more examples, see our Teacher's Guide.

Literature Group Week 2– Aphrodite
Day 2

Focus Virtue: Compassion is feeling sorry for those who are suffering and wanting to help.

Focus Vice: Indifference is ignoring the suffering or needs of others.

DISCUSS:

- Review the concepts "compassion" and "indifference". Ask the children to tell back the story of Aphrodite. Recall as many details as you can. Review the memory sentence from the day before.

- Review the memory sentences presented in the previous session.

FOLLOW-UP ACTIVITIES:

1. DICTATION:

- Individual or in Teams

- We divide the dictation sentences into three increasing levels of difficulty: pre-k and kindergarten, early elementary, and later elementary. For pre-K and kindergarten, rather than writing out a sentence, children are given a dictation sheet which simply has a choice of letters for four items. The instructor reads the word and students circle or underline the letter choice, which shows the sound the word starts with. See the dictation worksheet in the Appendix for pre-k and kindergarten.

- For children who can write and spell, repeat the sentence or sentences a few times, speaking slowly and clearly to give them plenty of time to get it down as accurately as possible.

- Students can record their dictation in the "dictation" section of the Year One Elementary Literature Workbook.

- To make this into a game, divide the children into teams. They will do their dictation exercise separately at first, but each person on the team who gets the dictation correct will get two points. Team members who make mistakes will get one point for their efforts. Before the instructor writes the correct sentence on the board, consider allowing team members to review each other's work and discuss corrections. This way, the children can help each other and each team maximizes their number of points.

Pre-K

- Aphrodite - begins with N, B, A, or L
- Melanion - begins with M, P, O, or U
- Race - begins with D, R, Q, or S
- Golden - begins with P, K, V, or G

Early Elementary

- Aphrodite had compassion for Melanion.

Later Elementary

- Aphrodite is the Greek goddess of love. Aphrodite had compassion for Melanion. She helped him win a race against Atalanta.

2. CREATIVE WRITING:

- Go back to the brainstorming page with the word bank and complete that if there's still more to be done. If it was completed in the last session, then introduce a creative writing activity. Have the students use the descriptive word bank to rewrite the story in either narrative or poem form. For poems, use the haiku form and show them the sample haiku based on some of the words from the brainstorming exercise. Each child's narration or poetry should be written into their individual narration notebook. If the child is too young to write, they can dictate to an adult who writes for them.

3. CLOSING GAME SUGGESTIONS:

- Number Knockout - links and explanations of this game can be found in our Teacher's Guide book, available for purchase on our website.
- Review games - these include Latin and other review games for our literature curriculum. For example, use 3x5 cards. Put the names of the gods and goddesses on one side of the card and what they are known for on a separate 3x5 card. Throughout the weeks, you can review the gods and goddesses by matching the name of the god or goddess with what they are known for. For more ideas, see our Teacher's Guide.

Literature Group Week 2– Aphrodite
Day 3

REVIEW: Review the concepts of compassion and indifference. Use the memory cards created for the previous session. Ask the students to recall the memory sentence for this story.

MEMORIZE:

Introduce the poem below, which students can memorize as a way of remembering the key aspects of the story. The text can be recited as poetry, or it can be rapped or sung if the students would like to add melody or beats.

The Goddess Demeter

Adorned with roses, dressed in pink,
Flowing with beauty after every blink
As gentle as doves in the skies above,
Aphrodite was the goddess of beauty and love
As gentle as the petals of lovely flowers,
Her mission was always to uplift and empower,
Determined to save Atalanta's fate,
Aphrodite vowed to bring love, not hate.
Atalanta was determined never to get married.
She was the fastest runner and knew the power she carried.
In the race for her heart, countless princes tried,
But each one lost and was sentenced to die!
Until one day, Prince Melonian approached,
Aphrodite decided to become his coach.
She gave him gold to win Atalanta's heart,
So the two fell in love and would never part.

FOLLOW-UP ACTIVITIES:

1. CREATIVE WRITING:

- Continue to work with the children on their own original poetry based on the story. (Use the word bank created earlier in the week.)

- Have older children work on writing their own version of the Demeter story with illustrations. This is best done in their individual notebook, lined on one side and blank on the other. See the Appendix for photos of this kind of notebook with sample student writing and illustrations. Or, record the student's poem in Nyansa's Year One Literature Workbook.

- Close out the story by inviting students to present the poetry, pictures, and/or other writing they have done this week.

2. CLOSING GAME SUGGESTIONS:

- Number Knockout - links and explanations of this game can be found in our Teacher's Guide book, available for purchase on our website.

- Review games - these include Latin and other review games for our literature curriculum. For example, use 3x5 cards. Put the names of the gods and goddesses on one side of the card and what they are known for on a separate 3x5 card. Throughout the weeks, you can review the gods and goddesses by matching the name of the god or goddess with what they are known for. For more ideas, see our Teacher's Guide.

Literature Group Week 2- Aphrodite Day 4

See Learning Through Art

On day four, we encourage you to use the Nyansa Art Curriculum. Students will learn to build observation skills and habits of attention. They will also engage in group discussions that discuss our virtues for the week.

If you do not have the Nyansa Year One Art Curriculum, you can use the illustrations from this week's lessons. Have your students look at the illustration for 2 minutes. After the two minutes, turn over the page. Ask your student to describe the illustration back to you without looking at the picture. Then, discuss how the illustrations for this week tell the story of this week's Greek Myth through the images they observed.

Literature Group Week 3- Ares
Day 1
Lesson 1: Ares - Greek God of War

Focus Virtue: Forgiveness is not holding someone else's bad actions against them.

Focus Vice: Vengeance is trying to make someone suffer because of their actions towards you

Today, we will be discussing forgiveness and vengeance. Discuss what each means. Create a new memory card for each term with its meaning and its opposite on the back of the card. These can be used for memory-matching games once there are enough of them. Identify themes that go with the story and write terms and definitions on flash cards. Introduce the story of Ares by allowing the students two minutes to examine her portrait. Then, turn over the portrait and ask the students to recall what they saw. Use the portrait discussion and the following facts to introduce the story:

Introduction:

Ares was the Greek god of war, courage, vengeance, and bloodthirstiness. He delighted in violence, conflict, revenge, and the destruction of battle. In many Greek stories, he would give those he liked courage, but not the steady sort of courage that helps people suffer and endure and love people in difficult circumstances, but the kind of courage that helps people fight and battle and do violence to others. Ares was the sort of god who could give you the courage to punch someone who had insulted you, but not the type of courage to admit you had been wrong. Bad-tempered and quarrel-loving, Ares's whole existence was devoted to violence. In art, the Greeks always drew Ares with weapons - either an entire set of armor or a simple spear and a peaked warrior's helmet. He was the son of Zeus and Hera, the king and queen of heaven, and his special animals were the snake and the vulture, an ill-omen of war and death. While the other gods would fight when they had a strong reason to, Ares loved fighting itself. He loved bloodshed so much that even his parents hated him. His children included the gods of fear and terror, Deimos and Phobos.

READ:

Read the story of Penthesilea (Greek Gods #3). Encourage narration activities as students listen (drawing, writing, etc).

Penthesilea

     Many Greek legends and myths surround one particularly famous war - the Trojan War - which was an ancient war between the Greeks and the Trojans. The Trojan War started when a Trojan prince, Paris, stole Helen, the wife of the Greek king Melenaus, and brought her home to Troy. Menelaus gathered up his troops and the other kings in the area, and together, they waged war on Troy for ten years, to the delight of cruel Ares. Among the Greek leaders were heroes like the half-god Achilles, who was the greatest warrior the world had ever seen, Odysseus, a king of crafty wisdom, and Ajax, the fierce giant. Priam, the king of the Trojans, was supported by his oldest son, the valiant Hector, and by the son of Aphrodite, brave Aeneas. The gods also took sides and interfered on one side or the other as the war went on. At one point, Prince Hector killed Achilles' best friend, Patroclus. This so infuriated Achilles that he challenged Hector in battle. Hector was good and brave, but he could not match Achilles for strength and skill, so Achilles killed him and then, in his anger, dishonored his body by dragging it through the dirt. Crushed and grieving, King Priam came to Achilles in the dead of night and begged him to give him his son back. Achilles agreed, and the heartbroken Trojans prepared to bury Hector.

`One of Ares' children, Penthesilea, was Queen of the Amazons, a race of fighting women who lived without men. She was a fierce warrior, skilled in fighting, and she, like her father, delighted in the thrill of violence and battle. When she heard about the Trojan War, she gathered up her warrior maidens, and together, they journeyed to Troy to help King Priam. As she arrived, they were burying the body of beloved Hector.

Priam threw a banquet for Penthesilea, welcoming her as if she had been his own daughter. Penthesilea felt sorry for the king, and her heart thirsted for the glory of battle, so she boasted at the table about how she would take the field in Hector's place and lead the Trojans to victory. The daughter of the god of war himself would surely triumph over Achilles!

But in the crowd sat Andromache, Hector's widow, gently rocking their baby. Andromache sat silently in sadness, not eating or drinking, fighting back the tears. She shook her head sadly over Penthesilea's vain boasting and warlike spirit.

"Does she think she can kill Achilles when she is not HALF the warrior my brave Hector was?" wondered Andromache in her heart. "She is doomed if she walks onto that field." And though Andromache's heart yearned to put the proud queen in her place, she knew that it would be no use, and so she sat and mourned the loss and destruction of war.

That night, Penthesilea went to bed happy, eager for war in the morning. Clever Athena, who had taken the Greek's side, sent the woman false dreams. Athena pretended to be Ares and told Penthesilea that she, his beloved daughter, would indeed conquer Achilles and win undying glory. In the morning, confident of victory, Penthesilea put on the gorgeous armor her father had given her - a glittering sword, chain mail that shone like a rainbow, and a golden shield. With confidence and glee, she led her maidens out onto the field of battle, ready to take revenge for Hector's death. Priam prayed to Zeus, asking him to help Ares' daughter in the coming fight. Mounted on a shining horse, Penthesilea rode up to the Greek troops and issued a challenge.

"Come on out and fight, you sniveling Greeks!" yelled Penthesilea, "And I will destroy you. Not one of you will go home to parents or wives or children, but the vultures will eat you all! You will pay for the horrible way you treated Hector. Where is Big Bad Ajax? Where is glittering Achilles? Come fight me, you cowards!"

With these words, Ares' daughter took the field, and the Greeks fled before her. Wherever she threw her spear, a man fell dead. For a while, it looked as if she would indeed conquer as man after man fell before the fierce Amazon warriors. Brave Penthesilea fought her way through the Greeks until she reached the beach where their boats were docked. By this time, the din of battle had reached Achilles, and when he realized the boats were threatened, he quickly put on his armor and went to join the fight.

Penthesilea saw him coming from far off, for his armor was god-given, and it gleamed like the sun. Her heart jumped with gladness, and she rushed towards him. But it was no contest. With one throw of his spear, god-like Achilles had pierced her heart, and she fell off her horse, dead. Achilles came towards her to see whom he had killed, and his heart was filled with grief. She was so beautiful in death, almost like a goddess lying asleep, that Achilles fell in love with her, and he grieved that she had died in battle. How horrible it was to have killed so beautiful a thing. Achilles respected her valor, and he feared the wrath of Ares, so he brought her back to the Trojans gently and allowed them to bury her with honor.

When Ares heard that Achilles had killed his war-like daughter, he sped towards Troy, bringing storms and destruction with him. He planned to take revenge on Achilles and make the Greeks pay for killing his beloved child. But when he reached the plains of Troy, Zeus surrounded Ares with thunder and lightning, and Ares was forced to stop. Zeus forbade Ares from taking vengeance - the war was bad enough. Ares knew he could not beat the all-powerful Zeus. No one could. Rather than be destroyed by his father, Ares held back, but his heart seethed with rage at the destruction of his daughter. Down below, the cycle of death and vengeance continued, and Ares had to be content with enjoying the suffering that surrounded him.

- *After narration activities are completed, have children practice saying the memory sentence for the story.*
- *Discuss children's responses to the discussion questions provided with the story, and/or create your own discussion questions.*
- *Copywork, poetry and brainstorming, and dictation activity worksheets are available in our Year One Elementary Literature Workbook. See our website for more information.*

DISCUSS:

Discussion Questions:

1. Who demonstrated vengeance in this story? Did anyone show forgiveness?

2. What could have happened if the characters in this story had chosen to show forgiveness instead of taking vengeance?

3. Trace the story of violence - who was the first person to be offended? How many people died because people kept taking revenge?

4. Why did Penthesilea get involved with the Trojan War?

5. Why was Andromache so sad?

6. Have you ever had to choose between forgiveness and vengeance? What did you choose?

MEMORY:

Memory Sentence: Ares' daughter Penthesilea tried to take revenge on Achilles but failed.

FOLLOW-UP ACTIVITIES:

1. **DRESS UP**

   - Have the children act out the story. Keeping a dress-up box with items that go with the story allows the children to act the story out with relevant props. Suggested dress-up items:

tiara (Penthesilea)	veil (Andromache)
various weaponry Amazons/ Greeks)	baby doll (Andromache)
spear/helmet (Ares)	crown (King Priam)
golden shield (Achilles)	cups

2. **BRAINSTORM**

   - Print out the full-page image of Ares, which is in the Appendix. Tape or glue this image to a large piece of planning paper. You will work with the children to brainstorm descriptive words that go along with the story of Penthesilea. These words will become a word bank that the children will use to write poetry, narrative summaries, etc. When writing poetry, the haiku poetry form is ideal as it is simple and allows for reinforcing the idea of syllables for young children.

- Here below are some words that work for the main characters and places mentioned in the story. Feel free to let the kids come up with their own words, but if they're having trouble, you can get things going by suggesting some on the lists below. Write the main persons, places, and things from the story up on a whiteboard or paper with space beneath them. Brainstorm descriptive words to go under each OR have descriptive words written in advance on stickies for younger kids. In the case of younger children, call out each term and ask for a student volunteer to put each term under the person, place, or thing that it describes. Keep this for the next session.

People
- Ares - cruel, bad tempered, war-going, bloodthirsty, angry, avenging, hated
- Penthesilea - warlike, brave, promising, avenging, bloodthirsty, taunting, proud, foolish, deceived, killed, mourned
- Achilles - strong, god-like, brave, winning, mourning, regretful
- Andromache - mourning, sad, loving, grieving, wise
- Hector - brave, strong, good, honest, faithful
- Priam - old, wise, welcoming, worried, grieving
- Zeus - powerful, restraining, fearsome
- Paris - thief, troublemaker
- Menelaus - husband, angry, vengeful
- Helen - stolen, beautiful

Things
- Troy - city, stronghold, unassailable
- Penthesilea's armor - gleaming, rainbow-like, shining, glittering
- Achille's armor - shining, golden, deadly

- When you finish this brainstorming, be sure to keep the large planning paper with all of the different words on it. This should be posted on the wall if possible so it can be a continued point of reference. This will be useful in helping children to remember the story and will act as the word bank for their poetry.

- Use the Nyansa Year One Literature Workbook and have students record the brainstorming words in the "brainstorming" section.

For more examples, see our Teacher's Guide.

Literature Group Week 3– Ares
Day 2

Focus Virtue: Forgiveness is not holding someone else's bad actions against them.

Focus Vice: Vengeance is trying to make someone suffer because of their actions towards you

DISCUSS:

- Review the concepts of "forgiveness" and "vengeance". Ask the children to tell back the story of Aphrodite. Recall as many details as you can. Review the memory sentence from the day before.

- Review the memory sentences presented in the previous session.

FOLLOW-UP ACTIVITIES:

1. DICTATION:

- Individual or in Teams

- We divide the dictation sentences into three increasing levels of difficulty: pre-k and kindergarten, early elementary, and later elementary. For pre-K and kindergarten, rather than writing out a sentence, children are given a dictation sheet, which simply has a choice of letters for four items. The instructor reads the word, and students circle or underline the letter choice, which shows the sound the word starts with. See the dictation worksheet in the Appendix for pre-k and kindergarten.

- For children who can write and spell, repeat the sentence or sentences a few times, speaking slowly and clearly to give them plenty of time to get it down as accurately as possible.

- Students can record their dictation in the "dictation" section of the Year One Elementary Literature Workbook.

- To make this into a game, divide the children into teams. They will do their dictation exercise separately at first, but each person on the team who gets the dictation correct will get two points. Team members who make mistakes will get one point for their efforts. Before the instructor writes the correct sentence on the board, consider allowing team members to review each other's work and discuss corrections. This way, the children can help each other and each team maximizes their number of points.

Pre-K

- Penthesilea - begins with P, Q, H, or L
- Troy - begins with M, L, E, or T
- Achilles - begins with D, A, S, or R
- War - begins with P, W, O, or U

Early Elementary

- Penthesilea tried to fight Achilles.

Later Elementary

- Ares's daughter Penthesilea loved war.
- Penthesilea tried to take vengeance on Achilles.
- Achilles won the battle, and Ares was filled with rage.

2. CREATIVE WRITING:

- Go back to the brainstorming page with the word bank and complete that if there's still more to be done. If it was completed in the last session, then introduce a creative writing activity. Have the students use the descriptive word bank to rewrite the story in either narrative or poem form. For poems, use the haiku form and show them the sample haiku based on some of the words from the brainstorming exercise. Each child's narration or poetry should be written into their individual narration notebook. If the child is too young to write, they can dictate to an adult who writes for them.

3. CLOSING GAME SUGGESTIONS:

- Number Knockout - links and explanations of this game can be found in our Teacher's Guide book, available for purchase on our website.
- Review games - these include Latin and other review games for our literature curriculum. For example, use 3x5 cards. Put the names of the gods and goddesses on one side of the card and what they are known for on a separate 3x5 card. Throughout the weeks, you can review the gods and goddesses by matching the name of the god or goddess with what they are known for. For more ideas, see our Teacher's Guide.

Literature Group Week 3– Ares
Day 3

REVIEW: Review the concepts of forgiveness and vengeance. Use the memory cards created for the previous session. Ask the students to recall the memory sentence for this story.

MEMORIZE:

Introduce the poem below, which students can memorize as a way of remembering the key aspects of the story. The text can be recited as poetry, or it can be rapped or sung if the students would like to add melody or beats.

Ares

Greek god of vengeance, courage, and war,
Never remembering what he was truly fighting for,
Too blinded by pride to admit when he was wrong,
Ares loved bloodshed like birds love songs.

The great Trojan War lasted 10 years.
Filled with much pain, turmoil, and tears.
Penthesilea, Ares's own flesh and blood,
Was too eager to battle amongst swords and mud.

She boasted that she could defeat each and every Greek,
She sought the most glory that a god could seek.
But she was quickly humbled when it was time for war,
When Achilles came with power, she had never seen before.

Upon hearing of the terrible tragedy with his daughter,
Ares summoned the rage of a father
He brought more destruction to the city of Troy
Vengeance was the only source of his joy.

FOLLOW-UP ACTIVITIES:

1. CREATIVE WRITING:

- Continue to work with the children on their own original poetry based on the story. (Use the word bank created earlier in the week.)

- Have older children work on writing their own version of the Demeter story with illustrations. This is best done in their individual notebook, lined on one side and blank on the other. See the Appendix for photos of this kind of notebook with sample student writing and illustrations. Or, record the student's poem in Nyansa's Year One Literature Workbook.

- Close out the story by inviting students to present the poetry, pictures, and/or other writing they have done this week.

2. CLOSING GAME SUGGESTIONS:

- Number Knockout - links and explanations of this game can be found in our Teacher's Guide book, available for purchase on our website.

- Review games - these include Latin and other review games for our literature curriculum. For example, use 3x5 cards. Put the names of the gods and goddesses on one side of the card and what they are known for on a separate 3x5 card. Throughout the weeks, you can review the gods and goddesses by matching the name of the god or goddess with what they are known for. For more ideas, see our Teacher's Guide.

Literature Group Week 3– Ares
Day 4

See Learning Through Art

On day four, we encourage you to use the Nyansa Art Curriculum. Students will learn to build observation skills and habits of attention. They will also engage in group discussions that discuss our virtues for the week.

If you do not have the Nyansa Year One Art Curriculum, you can use the illustrations from this week's lessons. Have your students look at the illustration for 2 minutes. After the two minutes, turn over the page. Ask your student to describe the illustration back to you without looking at the picture. Then, discuss how the illustrations for this week tell the story of this week's Greek Myth through the images they observed.

Literature Group Week 4– Hera
Day 1
Lesson 1: Hera - Greek Queen of the Gods

Focus Virtue: Kindness is treating others with respect, gentleness, and compassion.

Focus Vice: Cruelty is hurting others on purpose.

Today, we will be discussing forgiveness and vengeance. Discuss what each means. Create a new memory card for each term with its meaning and its opposite on the back of the card. These can be used for memory-matching games once there are enough of them. Identify themes that go with the story and write terms and definitions on flash cards. Introduce the story of Hera by allowing the students two minutes to examine her portrait. Then, turn over the portrait and ask the students to recall what they saw. Use the portrait discussion and the following facts to introduce the story:

Introduction:

Do you have anyone in your life who is constantly upset? The Greeks did! Hera, the queen of the gods and the goddess of women, marriage, and the stars, was always angry. In fairness to her, she had a lot of reasons to be angry. When she was born, her father, Cronos, swallowed her whole, along with all the rest of her brothers and sisters. Zeus freed her eventually, but then he made her marry him, even though she really didn't want to. After they were married, Zeus was a terrible husband. He was always falling in love with other people, which hurt Hera's feelings and made her jealous and angry. Still, it is hard to love people who are always angry, and the Greeks don't seem to have loved Hera very much.

Despite all her angry ways, the Greeks agreed that Hera was very beautiful, with large eyes. She was tall and graceful, every inch a queen. Her favorite animals were cows and peacocks. In ancient times, as in some cultures today, married women often wore veils over their heads, and often, the Greeks drew Hera wearing a veil since she was married. On her head, she also wore a crown, and she held a scepter to show that she was a queen. Together, Hera and Zeus had three children - Ares god of war, Hebe goddess of youth, and Eileithyia goddess of childbirth.

READ:

Read the story of Hera and Hephaestus (Greek Gods #4). Encourage narration activities as students listen (drawing, writing, etc).

Hera and Hephaestus

Hera's husband, Zeus, fell in love with a human princess named Io. Hera got very suspicious and followed Zeus one day. Clever Zeus realized his wife knew about this princess, so he turned Io into a beautiful white cow. Hera was not fooled, but she pretended to love the cow and asked for it as a present. Worried his wife would be suspicious if he refused, Zeus gave her the cow. Hera hated Zeus for loving other women, especially mere human girls, but she was too weak to fight him. Hera decided to punish the girl instead. She sent stinging flies to bite and sting it day after day until the cow went mad. Eventually, the other gods rescued Io, but Zeus continued being a bad husband, and Hera continued being cruel and angry.

Zeus had many other children. His most famous child was Athena. She didn't have a mother. Instead, one day, Zeus had a horrible headache. It got worse and worse, and then out jumped Athena from his forehead, full-grown and armed! Because she was born from his head, she had his wisdom and became known as the goddess of wisdom. Athena's full story is for another day. The point is that Hera was extremely jealous of Zeus for having such an amazing child all by himself.

Hera's jealousy inspired her to have a child by herself too, and eventually, she gave birth to the god of fire, Hephaestus. But he wasn't beautiful and wise. He wasn't handsome and strong. He didn't seem godlike in any way. He was extremely clever, but his mother couldn't see it. He just seemed small and weak, like the flame of a candle. Hera was embarrassed. This was the baby who was supposed to make Zeus jealous? Who would want such a child? Hera was so disgusted with him that she threw him down to the earth, which broke his legs. Angered and filled with shame, Hera decided to pretend the baby wasn't hers and went about her business. The baby Hephaestus lay wounded on the earth, but kind Thetis, goddess of the ocean, and Eurynome, goddess of watery meadows, took compassion on him and raised him themselves. For years, he lived with them and used his fire to make them beautiful things. As he grew, the god of fire learned the skill of metalworking until he was clever enough to make the most amazing things with his fiery forge.

As revenge for his mother's cruelty, he made her a golden chair and sent it to her as a present. Delighted with the gift, Hera sat upon it, not realizing that Hephaestus had enchanted it! The magical chair flipped Hera upside down and held her prisoner there! When Zeus demanded that Hephaestus free his mother, Hephaestus angrily replied that he had no mother. Eventually, the god Dionysus came to Hephaestus and convinced him to free Hera from her prison.

Perhaps Hera was sorry she had rejected such a gifted and clever son, for they seem to have lived as mother and son from then on.

Cultural Note: *Metalworking requires heating metal to very high temperatures, usually using a forge, which is a special kind of oven. The heat makes the metal soft enough to twist into different shapes. To make the metal strong again, the metal worker cools the metal very quickly in cold water. In the story of Hera and Hephaestus, Hera throws Hephaestus down to Thetis, who raises him. In other words, Hera throws her son, a fiery metal, into the ocean (represented by Thetis), which causes the fiery metal to grow strong as the water cools his flame. The story actually explains how metalworking works!*

- *After narration activities are completed, have children practice saying the memory sentence for the story.*
- *Discuss children's responses to the discussion questions provided with the story, and/or create your own discussion questions.*
- *Copywork, poetry, brainstorming, and dictation activity worksheets are available in our Year One Elementary Literature Workbook. See our website for more information.*

DISCUSS:

Discussion Questions:

1. Who demonstrated cruelty in this story? What motivated them to act in this way?
2. Who demonstrated kindness in this story? What motivated them to act this way?
3. What do you think might have happened if Hera had decided to love Hephaestus?
4. What do you think of Hephaestus' statement that he didn't have a mother? Who was his mother in the story?
5. Have you ever known anyone who was mean, or even cruel, to others? Why do you think they act that way?
6. Do you know anyone who is always kind? Why do you think they are so kind?

MEMORY:

Memory Sentence: Hera cruelly rejected her own son Hephaestus because he was lame.

FOLLOW-UP ACTIVITIES:

1. **DRESS UP**

   - Have the children act out the story. Keeping a dress-up box with items that go with the story allows the children to act the story out with relevant props. Suggested dress-up items:

crown	chair
veil	white blanket (Io)
scepter	crutches (Hephaestus)
fake fire	

2. **BRAINSTORM**

   - Print out the full-page image of Hera, which is in the Appendix. Tape or glue this image to a large piece of planning paper. You will work with the children to brainstorm descriptive words that go along with the story of Hera and Hephaestus. These words will become a word bank that the children will use to write poetry, narrative summaries, etc. When writing poetry, the haiku poetry form is ideal as it is simple and allows for reinforcing the idea of syllables for young children.

- When you finish this brainstorming, be sure to keep the large planning paper with all of the different words on it. This should be posted on the wall if possible so it can be a continued point of reference. This will be useful in helping children to remember the story and will act as the word bank for their poetry.

- Use the Nyansa Year One Literature Workbook and have students record the brainstorming words in the "brainstorming" section.

For more examples, see our Teacher's Guide.

People

- Hera - spiteful, vengeful, cruel, angry, disappointed, unloved, beautiful hurt, vindictive

- Zeus - unfaithful, unkind, deceptive, transforming

- Io - loved, changed, hidden, tormented, maddened, freed

- Athena - strong, glorious, wise, full-grown, armed

- Hephaestus - weak, small, fiery, clever, abandoned, saved, cherished, grown, angry, vengeful, master craftsman

- Thetis and Eurynome - kind, protective, saving

Things

- Golden chair - beautiful, deceptive, imprisoning

Literature Group Week 4– Hera
Day 2

Focus Virtue: Kindness is treating others with respect, gentleness, and compassion.

Focus Vice: Cruelty is hurting others on purpose.

DISCUSS:

- Review the concepts of "kindness" and "cruelty". Ask the children to tell back the story of Aphrodite. Recall as many details as you can. Review the memory sentence from the day before.

- Review the memory sentences presented in the previous session.

FOLLOW-UP ACTIVITIES:

1. DICTATION:

- Individual or in Teams

- We divide the dictation sentences into three increasing levels of difficulty: pre-k and kindergarten, early elementary, and later elementary. For pre-K and kindergarten, rather than writing out a sentence, children are given a dictation sheet, which simply has a choice of letters for four items. The instructor reads the word, and students circle or underline the letter choice, which shows the sound the word starts with. See the dictation worksheet in the Appendix for pre-k and kindergarten.

- For children who can write and spell, repeat the sentence or sentences a few times, speaking slowly and clearly to give them plenty of time to get it down as accurately as possible.

- Students can record their dictation in the "dictation" section of the Year One Elementary Literature Workbook.

- To make this into a game, divide the children into teams. They will do their dictation exercise separately at first, but each person on the team who gets the dictation correct will get two points. Team members who make mistakes will get one point for their efforts. Before the instructor writes the correct sentence on the board, consider allowing team members to review each other's work and discuss corrections. This way, the children can help each other and each team maximizes their number of points.

Pre-K

- Hera - begins with N, R, H, or L
- Zeus - begins with Z, P, O, or U
- Io- begins with B, R, Q, or I
- Athena - begins with P, K, A, or W

Early Elementary

- Hera cruelly abandoned Hephaestus.

Later Elementary

- Hera was jealous of Zeus. She gave birth to Hephaestus, but she did not love him. She cruelly abandoned him because he was weak.

2. CREATIVE WRITING:

- Go back to the brainstorming page with the word bank and complete that if there's still more to be done. If it was completed in the last session, then introduce a creative writing activity. Have the students use the descriptive word bank to rewrite the story in either narrative or poem form. For poems, use the haiku form and show them the sample haiku based on some of the words from the brainstorming exercise. Each child's narration or poetry should be written into their individual narration notebook. If the child is too young to write, they can dictate to an adult who writes for them.

3. CLOSING GAME SUGGESTIONS:

- Number Knockout - links and explanations of this game can be found in our Teacher's Guide book, available for purchase on our website.
- Review games - these include Latin and other review games for our literature curriculum. For example, use 3x5 cards. Put the names of the gods and goddesses on one side of the card and what they are known for on a separate 3x5 card. Throughout the weeks, you can review the gods and goddesses by matching the name of the god or goddess with what they are known for. For more ideas, see our Teacher's Guide.

Literature Group Week 4– Hera
Day 3

REVIEW: Review the concepts of forgiveness and vengeance. Use the memory cards created for the previous session. Ask the students to recall the memory sentence for this story.

MEMORIZE:

Introduce the poem below, which students can memorize as a way of remembering the key aspects of the story. The text can be recited as poetry, or it can be rapped or sung if the students would like to add melody or beats.

The Goddess Hera

Hera, the lovely, godly queen,
Was driven by anger and often mean.
After her father nearly took her life,
She was FORCED to become Zeus's wife.
Goddess of women, marriage, and the stars,
Her marriage felt like she was stuck behind bars.
With Zeus always longing for other women,
Anger and betrayal fueled her decisions.
When she found out Zeus had another love,
Unrest lingered in the skies above.
She even found out he had a child on his own,
Which made her feel even more caged and alone.
Hera gave birth to Hephaestus in spite,
But she banned and shamed him with all her might.
He grew up to be the mighty god of fire,
And got revenge on his mother and her bitter desire.

FOLLOW-UP ACTIVITIES:

1. CREATIVE WRITING:

- Continue to work with the children on their own original poetry based on the story. (Use the word bank created earlier in the week.)

- Have older children work on writing their own version of the story with illustrations. This is best done in their individual notebook, lined on one side and blank on the other. See the Appendix for photos of this kind of notebook with sample student writing and illustrations. Or, record the student's poem in Nyansa's Year One Literature Workbook.

- Close out the story by inviting students to present the poetry, pictures, and/or other writing they have done this week.

2. CLOSING GAME SUGGESTIONS:

- Number Knockout - links and explanations of this game can be found in our Teacher's Guide book, available for purchase on our website.

- Review games - these include Latin and other review games for our literature curriculum. For example, use 3x5 cards. Put the names of the gods and goddesses on one side of the card and what they are known for on a separate 3x5 card. Throughout the weeks, you can review the gods and goddesses by matching the name of the god or goddess with what they are known for. For more ideas, see our Teacher's Guide.

Literature Group Week 4– Hera
Day 4

See Learning Through Art

On day four, we encourage you to use the Nyansa Art Curriculum. Students will learn to build observation skills and habits of attention. They will also engage in group discussions that discuss our virtues for the week.

If you do not have the Nyansa Year One Art Curriculum, you can use the illustrations from this week's lessons. Have your students look at the illustration for 2 minutes. After the two minutes, turn over the page. Ask your student to describe the illustration back to you without looking at the picture. Then, discuss how the illustrations for this week tell the story of this week's Greek Myth through the images they observed.

Literature Group Week 5– Apollo
Day 1
Lesson 1: Apollo - Greek God of Music and Archery

Focus Virtue: Humility is acknowledging your own flaws and recognizing the gifts of others.

Focus Vice: Arrogance is thinking you are much better than other people.

Today, we will be discussing forgiveness and vengeance. Discuss what each means. Create a new memory card for each term with its meaning and its opposite on the back of the card. These can be used for memory-matching games once there are enough of them. Identify themes that go with the story and write terms and definitions on flash cards. Introduce the story of Apollo and Daphne by allowing the students two minutes to examine her portrait. Then, turn over the portrait and ask the students to recall what they saw. Use the portrait discussion and the following facts to introduce the story:

Use the following illustrations for this week.

READ:

Read the story of Apollo and Daphne (Greek Gods #5). Encourage narration activities as students listen (drawing, writing, etc).

Apollo and Daphne

Of Zeus' many children, perhaps the most revered among the Greeks was Apollo, the god of music, healing, and archery. The Greeks often depicted Apollo as a young, handsome man with long hair. In his hands, he often holds a bow and arrows or a lyre, which is a small harp. The Greeks had a myth that Apollo had invented the flute and that he played the lyre. On his head, the Greeks often drew him wearing a crown of laurel leaves. Often, before singing a song, the Greek poets would ask Apollo to bless them. It may seem odd that the god of archery would also be the god of healing, but the Greeks thought that Apollo carried out the punishments and rewards ordered by Zeus. Zeus was supposed to give out law and justice to both the gods and human beings, and they believed he would send out Apollo to either punish someone or to heal them, depending on what that person deserved. If anyone died suddenly, the Greeks thought Apollo was responsible.

Apollo was also the Greek god of prophecy (which means telling the future). In one of the most famous myths about Apollo, he struck down a great snake called Python, who guarded the oracle at Delphi and took control of the oracle. An oracle is a place where people went to hear the gods speak, and at Delphi, there were cracks in the ground where gasses would come up out of the earth. A priestess of Apollo would breathe in the gasses (which would make her kinda loopy), and then the Greeks would ask her questions. They believed her answers were prophecies and advice from Apollo, but usually, the advice was not very helpful.

Apollo was very proud of his archery skills - his deadly arrows never missed their targets. One day, as he sat stringing his strong bow, he saw Eros flying by. Winged Eros was the young god of love, son of Aphrodite, goddess of love, and he also had his bow and arrows with him. Now, Apollo used his arrows to destroy human beings, but Eros used his arrows to make people fall in love.

"Well, hello, little boy," jeered Apollo, "You look ridiculous holding that bow and arrows. You should leave the archery to men like me! Kids these days… you can't even really use that thing! All you can do is make people fall in love. I killed the famous Python, the huge horrible beast, with my bow and arrows. I am the best archer in the entire world, and you will never be as famous as me. Why bother even carrying your flimsy little bow?"

Young Eros looked at Apollo and smirked mischievously.

"Your bow may be the most powerful," said Eros, "but *I* will overpower *you*. Just you wait." And Eros sped away on his small wings. Apollo laughed scornfully to himself and forgot all about his conversation with Eros.

But the young god of love had a special plan cooked up for Apollo. With a quick pluck of his bow, he shot an arrow into the heart of the river nymph, Daphne. The fair nymph was the graceful daughter of the river Peneus. Anyone who looked at her fell in love with her, but Eros hit her with not the arrow of love but with the arrow of hate. It pierced her heart as she danced through the trees with her friends, and she immediately hated all men and announced that she would never marry! Then Eros turned and shot his bow at Apollo, but this time with an arrow of love. The arrow struck Apollo in the heart, and instantly, he fell desperately in love with Daphne.

So greatly did Apollo love Daphne that he set out to make her his wife immediately. Appearing as a handsome young man, Apollo tried to talk to Daphne, but she ran away from him, her hair ribbons streaming out behind her. He thought maybe some music would charm her, so he pulled out his flute and played the most beautiful music, but still she ran away.

"Come back!" called Apollo as he chased her, "I love you! Be my bride, my beautiful one! Don't be afraid of me! Do you know who chases you? It is I, Apollo, and you can never outrun me! Oh, be careful! You're going to trip and fall! Stop!"

But Eros' arrow had made Daphne fear Apollo, and she ran as fast as a terrified rabbit, dashing in between trees and through bushes. No matter how fast she ran, however, the ageless god ran faster. As she glanced behind her, she saw Apollo closing in on her. With a final burst of speed, she reached her father, the flowing river.

"Oh save me, Father!" she cried in terror, "Don't let him catch me!" And as the frightened girl spoke, she felt her arms fly upwards, and her feet sink into the ground. Her river father had heard her and transformed Daphne into a beautiful laurel tree!

Apollo reached her just as her slender arms transformed into leafy branches. The mighty god fell at her roots and cried, hugging her graceful trunk.

"I would have loved you forever," he cried, "I am terribly sad. For even though I am a healer, I cannot heal myself of this wound of love. Love makes the most horrible wounds of all."

And as Apollo mourned, the graceful laurel tree bent down her branches over him. Looking up, he took a small branch and wove it into a crown for his head.

"For now and for always, I will wear the laurel branches in honor of you, my true love," promised Apollo. And so the Greeks considered the laurel Apollo's special tree, and they rarely drew him without including a beautiful wreath of laurel upon his mighty head.

Cultural Note: Did you know that several of the first rockets NASA sent into space were called "Apollo"? The astronauts decided to name the rocket project after a Greek god or hero, and they chose Apollo. The rocket ship Apollo 11 was the first one with people in it to land on the moon.

After reading the story, do the following: narration, discussion, memory sentence, etc. For more information see the first four weeks instructions.

DISCUSS:

Discussion Questions:

1. How did Apollo act arrogantly? What was the consequence of his behavior? Did his boasting make Eros think better of him?
2. Apollo's arrows cause pain in people's bodies - what kind of pain did Eros' arrows create in Apollo?
3. Have you ever boasted to someone? What would be a better way to respond?
4. Daphne ended up as a tree in the story. Is this a fair ending for her? Did she do anything wrong? Is there an alternative ending you could imagine?
5. [Christian] The Greeks thought their god spoke to them through the oracle. How does God speak to us?

MEMORY:

Memory Sentence: Eros punished arrogant Apollo by making him fall in love.

FOLLOW-UP ACTIVITIES:

1. DRESS UP

- Have the children act out the story. Suggested dress-up items:

bow and arrows (Apollo)	wreath of leaves (representing laurel)
smaller bow and arrows (Eros)	ribbons (Daphne)

2. BRAINSTORM

- Print out the full-page image of Hera, which is in the Appendix. Tape or glue this image to a large piece of planning paper. Brainstorm words to describe the people, places, and things from the story. When writing poetry, the haiku poetry form is ideal as it is simple and allows for reinforcing the idea of syllables for young children.

- You can also replace "people" with characters, "things" with objects, and "places" with settings.

  For more information, see the brainstorming section in previous weeks.

People
- Apollo - arrogant, powerful, boastful, musical, gifted, talented, archer, wounded, in love, sad, healer
- Eros - young, mischievous, winged, offended, vengeful, clever
- Daphne - young, beautiful, graceful, nymph, frightened, quick, transformed

Places
- Forest - leafy, green, thicketed
- Oracles at Delphi - guarded, won by Apollo, mysterious, revered, religious

---

Literature Group Week 5– Apollo
Day 2

Focus Virtue: Humility is acknowledging your own flaws and recognizing the gifts of others.

Focus Vice: Arrogance is thinking you are much better than other people.

DISCUSS:

- Review the virtue and vice concepts. Have children narrate back the story from the previous day.
- Review the memory sentences presented in the previous session.

FOLLOW-UP ACTIVITIES:

1. DICTATION:

- Individual or in Teams - For more information, see previous weeks.

Pre-K

- Apollo- begins with M, D, A, or U
- Daphne- begins with I, O, P, or D
- Love - begins with H, L, R, or T
- Boastful - begins with B, K, S, or C

Early Elementary

- Apollo boasted about his archery skills to Eros.

Later Elementary

- Apollo boasted that he was a better archer than Eros. Eros shot Apollo with an arrow of love.
  Apollo fell in love with Daphne. Daphne turned into a tree in order to escape him.

2. CREATIVE WRITING:

- Go back to the brainstorming page with the word bank and complete that if there's still more to be done. If it was completed in the last session, then introduce a creative writing activity. Have the students use the descriptive word bank to rewrite the story in either narrative or poem form. For poems, use the haiku form and show them the sample haiku based on some of the words from the brainstorming exercise. Each child's narration or poetry should be written into their individual narration notebook. If the child is too young to write, they can dictate to an adult who writes for them.

3. CLOSING GAME SUGGESTIONS:

- Number Knockout - links and explanations of this game can be found in our Teacher's Guide book, available for purchase on our website.
- Review games - these include Latin and other review games for our literature curriculum. For example, use 3x5 cards. Put the names of the gods and goddesses on one side of the card and what they are known for on a separate 3x5 card. Throughout the weeks, you can review the gods and goddesses by matching the name of the god or goddess with what they are known for. For more ideas, see our Teacher's Guide.

Literature Group Week 5– Apollo
Day 3

REVIEW: Review the concepts for the virtues and vices. Use the memory cards created for the previous session. Ask the students to recall the memory sentence for this story.

MEMORIZE:

Introduce the poem below, which students can memorize as a way of remembering the key aspects of the story. The text can be recited as poetry, or it can be rapped or sung if the students would like to add melody or beats.

Apollo

Many say that the god Apollo,
Had a heart that wasn't full but hollow.
Skilled god of music and archery,
Apollo could also predict the future, telling the prophecies

Blessed with the accuracy of his bow and arrow,
His weapons hit their targets with the grace of a sparrow
He mocked young Eros for claiming his skills could compare,
But Eros simply plotted, with a plan and a glare.

One day, he shot Apollo with the arrow of love,
Forcing him to fall in love with Daphne, a river nymph above.
But Daphne was shot with the arrow of hate,
That would lead to the demise of Apollo's fate.

No matter how many times he tried and tried,
Each time Apollo courted Daphne, she would run away and hide!
She begged her father to turn her into a laurel tree,
Lonely and heartbroken would Apollo always be.

FOLLOW-UP ACTIVITIES:

1. CREATIVE WRITING:

- Continue to work with the children on their own original poetry based on the story. (Use the word bank created earlier in the week.)

- Have older children work on writing their own version of the story with illustrations. This is best done in their individual notebook, lined on one side and blank on the other. See the Appendix for photos of this kind of notebook with sample student writing and illustrations. Or, record the student's poem in Nyansa's Year One Literature Workbook.

- Close out the story by inviting students to present the poetry, pictures, and/or other writing they have done this week.

2. CLOSING GAME SUGGESTIONS:

- Number Knockout - links and explanations of this game can be found in our Teacher's Guide book, available for purchase on our website.

- Review games - these include Latin and other review games for our literature curriculum. For example, use 3x5 cards. Put the names of the gods and goddesses on one side of the card and what they are known for on a separate 3x5 card. Throughout the weeks, you can review the gods and goddesses by matching the name of the god or goddess with what they are known for. For more ideas, see our Teacher's Guide.

Literature Group Week 5– Apollo Day 4

See Learning Through Art

On day four, we encourage you to use the Nyansa Art Curriculum. Students will learn to build observation skills and habits of attention. They will also engage in group discussions that discuss our virtues for the week.

If you do not have the Nyansa Year One Art Curriculum, you can use the illustrations from this week's lessons. Have your students look at the illustration for 2 minutes. After the two minutes, turn over the page. Ask your student to describe the illustration back to you without looking at the picture. Then, discuss how the illustrations for this week tell the story of this week's Greek Myth through the images they observed.

Literature Group Week 6– Athena
Day 1
Lesson 1: Athena - Greek Goddess of Wisdom

Focus Virtue: Wisdom is knowing the right thing to do in every different situation.

Focus Vice: Foolishness is making bad decisions and ignoring good advice.

Discuss today's virtue and vice. Introduce the story of Athena and Arachne. For more details, see previous lessons.

Use the following illustrations for this week.

INTRODUCTION:

Have you ever had to make a difficult choice about something? Sometimes, it can be hard to know what the best thing to do is, especially if making the wrong choice could hurt people. The Greeks also faced many hard choices, and they had a special goddess to help them - Athena, the goddess of wisdom. In stories about her, Athena is often guiding, protecting, warning, and teaching heroes faced with difficult situations. According to myths, Zeus got a horrible headache one day. When he hit his head, it split open, and Athena popped out fully grown. The Greeks believed that Athena had Zeus' wisdom and that she often gave this wisdom to mortals. She also taught them how to tame horses and how to plow the fields for food. Among the animals, owls and snakes were considered sacred to her. On vases or in statue form, Athena is usually wearing a long sleeveless dress called a tunic, sometimes with armor on top of it. She often has a very serious expression, like she's thinking carefully about something.

The Greeks also considered Athena to be the goddess of war, but not in the same way Ares was. Athena was the goddess of <u>strategic</u> war, which is a war where you use your brains to fight as opposed to just relying on physical strength. One of the most popular legends about Athena says that she helped the hero Perseus defeat the snake-haired monster, Medusa, who could freeze a person to stone with one look at her awful eyes. As a thank you, Perseus gave the head of Medusa to Athena, who put it on her shield to frighten and destroy her enemies.

Athena was also famous for weaving, a skill she had gifted to humankind. Weaving was very important in the ancient world for making all kinds of cloth.

READ:

Read the story of Athena and Arachne (Greek Gods #6). Encourage narration activities as students listen (drawing, writing, etc).

Athena and Arachne

In the region of Lydia (which is in the modern country called Turkey) was a girl who wove beautiful clothes. Her name was Arachne, and she wasn't a princess. Her father had a wool-dying business, and they were common everyday folk, but she could weave so well that people came from miles around to watch her and to buy her wares. With quickness and grace, the girl would take wool from the sheep, spin it into yarn, weave it into cloth, and then embroider fabulous pictures all over the cloth. The people exclaimed, "You must have been taught by Athena herself! For no one could weave as well as you had not the goddess helped them!"

At this, Arachne should have praised Athena, for she knew that all good gifts come from the gods, but instead, she thrust out a proud chin and said, "Not me! I figured out how to weave all by myself! I am so good at my craft, I can weave better than the goddess herself!" And the girl's words spread throughout the region.

Athena heard what the girl was saying, and her heart was filled with anger. How dare the girl despise her, Athena, who taught the world to weave! But Athena never acted hastily or foolishly, so she dressed as an old woman and, pretending to hobble with a cane, walked into the shed where the girl wove her wares surrounded by admirers.

The girl saw the old woman and exclaimed, "Ah gray mother, have you come to see the cloth that is better than the cloth woven by the goddess herself?"

Athena's cold gray eyes looked over the girl. Then she spoke gently but firmly.

"There are many things about getting old that are difficult, but one nice thing is that you have wisdom and experience. Listen to me - you weave very well, but you should give credit to the goddess who gave you this gift! To speak against the gods is foolishness. Repent! Ask the goddess to forgive you your rash boastings, and I am sure she will forgive you!"

But the girl laughed in her face. "You are so old you can't even think anymore! Lecture your own children. I will take my own advice. If clever Athena wants to keep the weaving crown for herself, why doesn't she come to me and prove she can weave better than me!"

"She is here. Let us compete!" said Athena coldly, and as the astonished girl watched, the bent old woman in front of her transformed into the tall and graceful goddess. All the people who had been watching Arachne spin fell on their faces in reverence before the goddess, but Arachne just stood, head held high, her hand resting on her weaving loom.

"Fine!" she answered, her voice shaking just a little, "Let's compete!" With a wave of the hand, Athena summoned her loom, and the goddess and the girl began to weave.

Athena wove a picture that told the story of her contest with Poseidon for Athens. In the story, Poseidon had offered a well to the Athenians if they would worship him most of all. Athena offered them an olive tree instead, and they picked her as their own special goddess. Surrounding this beautiful and intricate picture was a rainbow with vibrant colors, and in the very center, the goddess had embroidered a graceful olive tree full of fruit. The edges gleamed with gold and silver threads so that they shimmered when it moved.

When she finished weaving, she looked over at Arachne's tapestry. The girl had woven pictures as well, but her pictures were insulting and not honoring. She had woven pictures of the gods disguised as animals trying to trick humans. Also, she had woven pictures of the gods fighting and bickering amongst themselves. Every picture was designed to mock and humiliate the gods. Along the entire edge, Arachne had woven beautifully intricate vines and flowers. Athena stared at the tapestry. Try as she might, she could find nothing wrong with it. It was absolutely gorgeous and horribly insulting.

Athena, the wise and powerful, turned to Arachne with a small, dangerous smile. "Well, girl," she said, "You have indeed woven well. And I will make sure you are known forever for your weaving, but you must pay for your rudeness to the gods above."

Athena grabbed the girl and threw her to the floor. The girl shrunk, her arms and legs doubled, and the thread she held attached itself to her back. With shock, the others in the room looked at what had been Arachne and instead saw a spider that crept slowly away into a corner to hide. So whenever you see a spider's web, think of Arachne, the famous spinner who was foolish enough to mock the gods!

Language Note: *All spiders and scorpions have the Latin scientific name "Arachnid." They are named that because of the famous story of Arachne!*

DISCUSS:

Discussion Questions:

1. How did Arachne act foolishly? How could she have made wiser choices?

2. Why do you think it's important that Arachne was from a common family, as opposed to being a princess?

3. Would Arachne have been punished if she had woven something less insulting to the gods? Did Arachne deserve the punishment that Athena gave her? Why or why not?

4. Has anyone ever given you a wise warning or good advice? Did you follow the advice? Or did you listen to the warning? What happened?

MEMORY:

Memory Sentence: Arachne foolishly mocked Athena.

FOLLOW-UP ACTIVITIES:

1. **DRESS UP**

   • Have the children act out the story. Suggested dress-up items:

thread	cane/walking stick
cloth	rubber spider
easels (for looms)	shield (Athena)
cloak	

2. **BRAINSTORM**

   • Use a full-color picture of Athena. Brainstorm words for the people (characters), places (setting), or things (objects) from the story. For more details, see previous lessons.

   People
   - Athena - wise, war-like, warning, furious, angry, crafty, giving, generous, punishing
   - Arachne - crafty, gifted, artistic, famous, foolish, haughty, proud, punished, spidery

   Things
   - Athena's tapestry - lovely, honoring, beautiful, glimmering, golden, celebratory
   - Arachne's tapestry - complicated, intricate, beautiful, shaming, rude, dishonoring

Literature Group Week 6– Athena
Day 2

Focus Virtue: Wisdom is knowing the right thing to do in every different situation.

Focus Vice: Foolishness is making bad decisions and ignoring good advice.

DISCUSS:

- Review the virtue and vice concepts. Have children narrate back the story from the previous day.
- Review the memory sentences presented in the previous session.

FOLLOW-UP ACTIVITIES:

1. DICTATION:

- Individual or in Teams - For more information, see previous weeks.

Pre-K

- Athena - begins with M, D, A, or P
- Spider - begins with N, O, P, or S
- Wisdom - begins with H, W, Q, or T
- Contest - begins with C, L, S, or I

Early Elementary

- Athena turned Arachne into a spider.

Later Elementary

- Arachne claimed she could weave better than Athena. When Athena challenged her to a contest, she wove rude stories into her tapestry. Athena punished her by turning her into a spider.

2. CREATIVE WRITING:

- Go back to the brainstorming page with the word bank and complete that if there's still more to be done. For more information, see previous lessons.

3. CLOSING GAME SUGGESTIONS:

Number Knockout/ Review Games. See previous lessons for more information.

Literature Group Week 6– Athena
Day 3

REVIEW: Review the concepts for the virtues and vices. Use the memory cards created for the previous session. Ask the students to recall the memory sentence for this story.

MEMORIZE:

Introduce the poem below, which students can memorize as a way of remembering the key aspects of the story. The text can be recited as poetry, or it can be rapped or sung if the students would like to add melody or beats.

The Goddess Athena

Treasured goddess of wisdom and war,
Blessed with the skills worth fighting for,
Born straight out of Zeus's head,
Athena was always one step ahead.

One day, she picked up her cloth to weave.
When she heard things, she could not believe.
A girl named Arachne was challenging her skill.
Ignoring that her talents came from the goddess's will.

So Athena came down in a tricky disguise,
Determined to hear Arachne's lies.
She revealed herself and challenged her to a test,
To see who could really weave the best.

Arachne couldn't manage to hide her disrespect.
Her weaving was filled with insult and neglect.
Athena wouldn't be insulted beside her,
So she punished Arachne, turning her into a spider!

FOLLOW-UP ACTIVITIES:

1. CREATIVE WRITING:

- Continue to work with the children on their own original poetry based on the story. (Use the word bank created earlier in the week.)

- Have older children work on writing their own version of the story with illustrations. This is best done in their individual notebook, lined on one side and blank on the other. See the Appendix for photos of this kind of notebook with sample student writing and illustrations. Or, record the student's poem in Nyansa's Year One Literature Workbook.

- Close out the story by inviting students to present the poetry, pictures, and/or other writing they have done this week.

2. CLOSING GAME SUGGESTIONS:

- Number Knockout - links and explanations of this game can be found in our Teacher's Guide book, available for purchase on our website.

- Review games - these include Latin and other review games for our literature curriculum. For example, use 3x5 cards. Put the names of the gods and goddesses on one side of the card and what they are known for on a separate 3x5 card. Throughout the weeks, you can review the gods and goddesses by matching the name of the god or goddess with what they are known for. For more ideas, see our Teacher's Guide.

Literature Group Week 6– Athena Day 4

See Learning Through Art

On day four, we encourage you to use the Nyansa Art Curriculum. Students will learn to build observation skills and habits of attention. They will also engage in group discussions that discuss our virtues for the week.

If you do not have the Nyansa Year One Art Curriculum, you can use the illustrations from this week's lessons. Have your students look at the illustration for 2 minutes. After the two minutes, turn over the page. Ask your student to describe the illustration back to you without looking at the picture. Then, discuss how the illustrations for this week tell the story of this week's Greek Myth through the images they observed.

Literature Group Week 7– Zeus
Day 1
Lesson 1: Zeus - Greek God of Heaven

Focus virtue: Justice is giving to each person what they deserve.

Focus vice: Injustice is keeping from others what rightfully belongs to them.

Discuss the virtue and what each means. Create a new memory card for each term with its meaning and its opposite on the back of the card. More details can be found in previous weeks. Introduce the story of Zeus and Tantalus by allowing the students two minutes to examine her portrait. Then, turn over the portrait and ask the students to recall what they saw. Use the portrait discussion and the following facts to introduce the story:

Use the following illustrations for this week.

INTRODUCTION:

Long ago, in the land of Greece, the people worshiped many gods, but the most powerful god of them all was Zeus. In their art, the Greeks often painted Zeus holding a lightning bolt, his favorite weapon. They would paint a noble wreath of olive leaves on his head and a proud eagle perched on his hand. The Greeks considered Zeus to be the king of all the gods, the god of sky and heaven, the god of law and justice, and the god of kings. Through war and great struggles, Zeus had claimed the throne on Mount Olympus, the bright home of the gods, and it was his job to punish evildoers and to settle arguments between the other gods and goddesses.

Read the story of Zeus and Tantalus (Greek Gods #7). Encourage narration activities as students listen (drawing, writing, etc).

Zeus and Tantalus

Once, there was a king named Tantalus who was so rich he could buy anything his heart desired. But he was a cruel man. Because of his wealth, he was famous, and even the gods took notice of him. Zeus invited the man to join the gods on Mount Olympus for a special dinner. Flattered, King Tantalus accepted. How special to eat with the gods themselves! How exciting it is to taste their food. When people heard about his special invitation, how envious they would be, and how important he would look!

At the dinner, Tantalus kept very quiet and listened to the gods and goddesses talk around him. Now, you may not know this yet, but it turns out that when someone is quiet, other people will often assume that they are wise, and this happened to Tantalus, In truth, he was trying to overhear what the gods were saying so he could gossip about them with his friends back home, but the gods and goddess mistook his quietness for wisdom and respect. They soon relaxed around him and did not notice when he stole some ambrosia - the sweet food of the gods! Before he left, Tantalus bowed to Zeus and invited them all to a supper at his house the following week.

Over the next few days, Tantalus mocked the gods of heaven and spilled their secrets to anyone who would listen, all while snacking on the stolen ambrosia. Little did he know that Zeus had already overheard his gossiping and noticed the stolen food.

But even this boasting and gossiping became boring after a few days, and Tantalus came up with a truly wicked idea. The gods claimed to know everything, but did they *really*? Wouldn't it be funny to trick them and then boast about it? He knew just how. With a cruel smile, he ordered his servants to bring his very own son, Pelops, down to the kitchen and cook him for dinner! He would fool the gods into eating a roasted person! King Tantalus had his great table laid with golden plates and sparkling glasses, all ready to fool his special guests.

Immediately, Zeus knew something was wrong. He looked at his plate and then stared up into Tantalus' face, his eyes glowing and glaring. The other gods and goddesses, seeing their king's fierce expression, froze and turned to look at Tantalus. All except Demeter. Her eyes were so clouded with tears that she had not seen Zeus' face, and without even thinking, she took a bite of the food.

"STOP!" bellowed Zeus. Demeter dropped her fork. She saw everyone looking at her in horror. Together, they turned angrily to glare at Tantalus. The King of the Gods rose, and he seemed to Tantalus to grow even taller and brighter. The eagle of Zeus flew into the room and rested on his outstretched hand. Zeus was ready to serve justice.

"Tantalus," said Zeus, "You are a wicked, cruel, thieving, murderer! You have mocked the gods, stolen their food, and killed your own child. Such wickedness can not go unpunished. But first, let us heal the boy. He did not deserve to die."

At this, the other gods arose and dumped all of their food onto the center of the table. Zeus spoke a word, and poof - the boy Pelops stood before them! Well, mostly. A chunk was missing from his shoulder because of the bite poor Demeter had eaten. Feeling very sorry for the boy, Demeter fashioned a shoulder for him out of beautiful ivory and made him well.

After this, Zeus dragged Tantalus down to the land of the dead, where he devised a special punishment for him. Tantalus was tied in such a way that he stood in a pool of water with a tree dangling sweet fruits overhead, but Zeus was clever in how he made the pool and the fruit. Whenever Tantalus opened his mouth to drink the water, it dried up, and whenever he lifted his head to eat the fruit, the tree would bend away from him. And so, for all time, King Tantalus would be hungry and thirsty, surrounded by water and food, but never able to taste them!

Cultural Note: *It might surprise you to know that we get the word "tantalize" from the punishment Zeus gave to Tantalus. Tantalizing someone is to offer them something they want but then take it away, just as Zeus placed food and drink near Tantalus, only to take them away as punishment for his cruelty and wickedness!*

DISCUSS:

Discussion Questions:

1. Did Tantalus deserve the punishment Zeus gave him?

2. Why do we often mistake silence for wisdom?

3. Who else did Zeus give justice to in this story? Was there anyone who deserved justice but didn't get it?

4. Have you ever known anyone who deserved a reward or a punishment but didn't get justice? How did that make you feel?

MEMORY:

Memory Sentence: Zeus justly punished Tantalus for his crimes.

FOLLOW-UP ACTIVITIES:

1. **DRESS UP**

    • Have the children act out the story. Suggested dress-up items:

cups/plates	golden crown (for Tantalus
lightning bolt (for Zeus)	play dough or marshmallows (ambrosia)
leaf crown (for Zeus)	fruit (to hang over Tantalus' head)

2. **BRAINSTORM**

    • Use a full-color picture of Zeus. Brainstorm words for the people (characters), places (setting), or things (objects) from the story. For more details, see previous lessons.

People
   • Zeus - King, god, careful, powerful, just, angry
   • Tantalus - king, rich, evil, cruel, thief, malicious, gossiper, punished
   • Demeter - sad, young, murdered, resurrected, eaten, healed

Places
   • Mount Olympus - lofty, beautiful, shining, high, heavenly
   • King Tantalus' Home - rich, impressive, decorated

Things
   • Ambrosia - delicious, stolen, god's food
   • Lightning - weapon, dangerous, bright, heavenly

Literature Group Week 7– Zeus
Day 2

Focus virtue: Justice is giving to each person what they deserve.

Focus vice: Injustice is keeping from others what rightfully belongs to them.

DISCUSS:

- Review the virtue and vice concepts. Have children narrate back the story from the previous day.

- Review the memory sentences presented in the previous session.

FOLLOW-UP ACTIVITIES:

1. DICTATION:

- Individual or in Teams - For more information, see previous weeks.

Pre-K

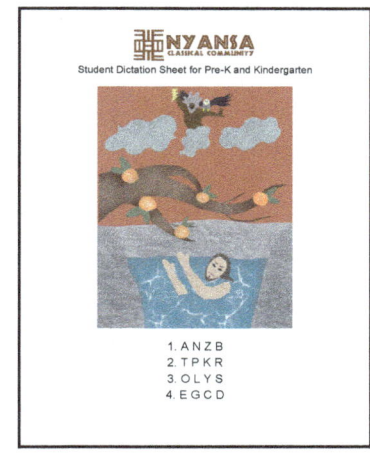

- Zeus - begins with A, N, Z, or B.
- Tantalus - begins with T, P, K, or R
- Olympus - begins with O, L, Y, or S
- Demeter - begins with E, G, C, or D

Early Elementary

- Zeus punishes unjust men.

Later Elementary

- Zeus is the king of the gods and upholds justice. Tantalus stole food from the gods and killed his own son. Zeus punishes Tantalus for his crimes.

2. CREATIVE WRITING:

- Go back to the brainstorming page with the word bank and complete that if there's still more to be done. For more information, see previous lessons.

3. CLOSING GAME SUGGESTIONS:

Number Knockout/ Review Games. See previous lessons for more information.

Literature Group Week 7- Zeus
Day 3

REVIEW: Review the concepts for the virtues and vices. Use the memory cards created for the previous session. Ask the students to recall the memory sentence for this story.

MEMORIZE:

Introduce the poem below, which students can memorize as a way of remembering the key aspects of the story. The text can be recited as poetry, or it can be rapped or sung if the students would like to add melody or beats.

King Zeus

There once was a king of many gods,
With strength and power from a lightning rod.
His knowledge of law and justice, put to use,
The god of Mount Olympus was named King Zeus!

There also was a king named Tantalus who lived in the lands of Earth,
He was an evil man, guided by greed and wealth since birth.
One day, after eating with the gods in heaven,
Tantalus was filled with a mind for aggression.

He would host a dinner for everyone,
And planned to serve plates of his very own son!
The gods were unaware of his trickery and spite,
Demeter even accidentally took a bite!

Zeus was outraged, as were the gods and his wife,
He quickly brought the poor boy back to life.
Determined to punish Tantalus for his horrendous crime,
Zeus sentenced him to be hungry and thirsty until the end of time.

FOLLOW-UP ACTIVITIES:

1. CREATIVE WRITING:

- Continue to work with the children on their own original poetry based on the story. (Use the word bank created earlier in the week.)

- Have older children work on writing their own version of the story with illustrations. This is best done in their individual notebook, lined on one side and blank on the other. See the Appendix for photos of this kind of notebook with sample student writing and illustrations. Or, record the student's poem in Nyansa's Year One Literature Workbook.

- Close out the story by inviting students to present the poetry, pictures, and/or other writing they have done this week.

2. CLOSING GAME SUGGESTIONS:

- Number Knockout - links and explanations of this game can be found in our Teacher's Guide book, available for purchase on our website.

- Review games - these include Latin and other review games for our literature curriculum. For example, use 3x5 cards. Put the names of the gods and goddesses on one side of the card and what they are known for on a separate 3x5 card. Throughout the weeks, you can review the gods and goddesses by matching the name of the god or goddess with what they are known for. For more ideas, see our Teacher's Guide.

Literature Group Week 7– Zeus
Day 4

See Learning Through Art

On day four, we encourage you to use the Nyansa Art Curriculum. Students will learn to build observation skills and habits of attention. They will also engage in group discussions that discuss our virtues for the week.

If you do not have the Nyansa Year One Art Curriculum, you can use the illustrations from this week's lessons. Have your students look at the illustration for 2 minutes. After the two minutes, turn over the page. Ask your student to describe the illustration back to you without looking at the picture. Then, discuss how the illustrations for this week tell the story of this week's Greek Myth through the images they observed.

Literature Group Week 8– Artemis
Day 1
Lesson 1: Artemis - Greek Goddess of Hunting

Focus Virtue: Gratitude is being thankful for all things and blessing others.

Focus Vice: Jealousy is hating others and wanting what they have for yourself.

Discuss the virtue and what each means. Create a new memory card for each term with its meaning and its opposite on the back of the card. More details can be found in previous weeks. Introduce the story of Artemis by allowing the students two minutes to examine her portrait. Then, turn over the portrait and ask the students to recall what they saw. Use the portrait discussion and the following facts to introduce the story:

Use the following illustrations for this week.

INTRODUCTION:

Artemis was the Greek goddess of hunting. This swift and graceful goddess was the daughter of Zeus and a Titaness named Leto. She was the twin sister of the god Apollo. She was very skilled with the bow and arrow, and like Apollo, she was thought to bring sudden healing or sudden death with her arrows. She was thought to love the forest and all wild animals. Deer were sacred to Artemis, and she was the patron goddess of young girls. In art, the Greeks depicted her as a beautiful young woman, graceful and slender, with a bow and quiver of arrows. Unlike Hera and Aphrodite, Artemis was a single goddess - she never married or had any children. She did, however, fall in love, as you are about to hear.

READ:

Read the story of Artemis (Greek Gods #8). Encourage narration activities as students listen (drawing, writing, etc).

Artemis

In all the history of the world, there never has been a man as handsome as the giant Orion. It was said he was so good-looking that the dawn herself fell in love with him. His head stood 70 feet above the earth, and his father, Poseidon, had granted him the gift of walking on water. Not only that, but he was a magnificent hunter, skilled with both a club and the bow and arrow. He was brave. He was strong. He was very tall. And Artemis fell in love with him.

They met in the forest on the island of Crete, where they both were hunting. Artemis was running through the woods with her nymphs and maidens when she came upon him, bow in hand, hunting the wild boar. It was love at first sight. With a twinkle in his eyes and a courteous bow, Orion asked to join Artemis' hunting party. Graciously, the goddess nodded her head, and together they sped through the woods. After that, Orion was her constant hunting companion. He considered himself her bodyguard, sworn to protect her with life and limb. For her part, Artemis had found a friend, a man she wished to live with forever. It was a happy time for her under the green leafy trees on the warm island.

But one person was not happy. The god Apollo was extremely jealous of Orion. Before this tall man had stolen his sister's attention, she had used to spend her time hunting with him! Now, she had no time for him, and even when she did talk to him, it was Orion this, Orion that - nothing but Orion. Sickening. Could Orion shoot nearly as well as divine Apollo? No! Was he as quick? Of course not. What did she see in him? Why did she abandon her brother and hunt with this mortal instead? It was embarrassing. Apollo missed his sister, and he hated Orion for stealing her time and attention.

One day, Apollo saw the giant taking a leisurely swim in the Mediterranean Sea as if it were his own private bathtub. Orion swam back and forth with graceful strokes, and Apollo was filled with disgust and rage. But then, an idea struck him, and he went in search of his sister. She was sitting in the woods, talking gently with a bear, and Apollo threw himself down beside her.

"Come on, Sis!" he said, "We haven't hunted together in ages. I bet you are getting rusty with only that Orion to hunt with. It's time you had some real competition! Why don't you come shooting with me?"

"Orion is a great hunter," sniffed Artemis, "but of course, I'd be happy to shoot with you. I have nothing else in particular going on today."

"I saw some rocks far out in the sea," said Apollo, "let's do some target practice." Artemis agreed, and brother and sister strolled down to the beach. Far, far away, a dark shape bobbed slowly on the surface of the water.

"See that rock way, way out there?" asked Apollo."

"Of course!" said Artemis.

"Well," taunted Apollo, "I bet you are so rusty from hanging out with mortals you can't hit it."

"Of course I can hit it, you ridiculous boy," said Artemis. She grabbed her bow, fit an arrow, took aim, and fired at the far-off object. It stopped bobbing and sank below the water.

"Ha! I told you I could hit it. Rusty am I?" laughed Artemis, "Admit it, brother! I am still a fabulous shot!"

Apollo grinned. "No doubt about it," he said, "that was a great shot. Well, I should be going!" And he sped off as fast as he could through the forest.

Artemis frowned as she watched him leave. Suddenly, something hit the back of her heel. She turned to look at the water, and there, at her feet, was the dead body of Orion, with her arrow through his head. With a cry of despair, she fell to the ground beside the body of her beloved. She wept and wept, cradling his head in her arms, but she could not bring him back to life.

Filled with fury, she swore revenge on her brother. Mustering her resolve, she dragged the body of Orion to the halls of Mount Olympus and placed him at the feet of Zeus. Tears spilled from her eyes as she told Zeus Almighty how Apollo had tricked her into killing her beloved. She told Zeus how splendid he had been, how mighty, how strong, how gifted. Although Zeus would not bring Orion back to life, he was not unmoved by her pleas. At her request, Zeus placed Orion among the stars to guard the heavens forever.

Cultural Note: If you ever look up in the night sky during the winter, you will see Orion in the sky even today. Look for his shiny belt, made up of three bright stars. Orion also holds a club and a lion's skin because of his skill as a hunter!

DISCUSS:

Discussion Questions:

1. Who showed jealousy in this story? Why was he jealous? What did his jealousy cause him to do?

2. How might this story have been different if Apollo had been thankful for what he had instead of focusing on what he had lost?

3. Would Orion have lived if Artemis hadn't spent so much time with him? What could she have done differently? How can you balance time spent with friends and family, to ensure everyone feels included? Is it always possible to give equal time to all the people in your life?

4. How did Apollo trick Artemis?

5. Did Orion deserve to die? Was what happened to him fair?

6. What are your thoughts on Zeus' decision? Should he have punished Apollo?

7. Have you ever been jealous of someone? What did you do?

MEMORY:

Memory Sentence: Artemis accidentally shot her beloved Orion.

FOLLOW-UP ACTIVITIES:

1. DRESS UP

- Have the children act out the story. Suggested dress-up items:

bow/arrows (Artemis)	another bow/harp (Apollo)
flower garlands (Artemis' nymphs)	crown (Zeus)
club/sword (Orion)	blue sheet (Mediterranean)
chairs (forest)	

2. BRAINSTORM

- Use a full-color picture of Artemis. Brainstorm words for the people (characters), places (setting), or things (objects) from the story. For more details, see previous lessons.

People
- Artemis - skilled, loving beautiful, gracious, tricked, grieved, mourning
- Orion - tall, strong, brave, handsome, murdered, mourned, honored, protective
- Apollo - jealous, cruel, crafty, plotting, muderous
- Zeus - all-powerful, just, vindicating

Places
- Crete - leafy, green, warm, pleasant, living, insular
- Mt. Olympus - lofty, shining, divine

Literature Group Week 8– Artemis
Day 2

Focus Virtue: Gratitude is being thankful for all things and blessing others.

Focus Vice: Jealousy is hating others and wanting what they have for yourself.

DISCUSS:

- Review the virtue and vice concepts. Have children narrate back the story from the previous day.

- Review the memory sentences presented in the previous session.

FOLLOW-UP ACTIVITIES:

1. DICTATION:

- Individual or in Teams - For more information, see previous weeks.

Pre-K

- Artemis - begins with B, D, A, or Q

- Hunting - begins with H, O, P, or U

- Trick- begins with I, R, E, or T

- Jealousy - begins with U, J, S, or E

Early Elementary

- Apollo tricked Artemis into killing Orion.

Later Elementary

- Artemis fell in love with Orion. Apollo was jealous of Orion. He tricked Artemis into shooting Orion. Zeus put Orion among the stars.

2. CREATIVE WRITING:

- Go back to the brainstorming page with the word bank and complete that if there's still more to be done. For more information, see previous lessons.

3. CLOSING GAME SUGGESTIONS:

Number Knockout/ Review Games. See previous lessons for more information.

Literature Group Week 8– Artemis
Day 3

REVIEW: Review the concepts for the virtues and vices. Use the memory cards created for the previous session. Ask the students to recall the memory sentence for this story.

MEMORIZE:

Introduce the poem below, which students can memorize as a way of remembering the key aspects of the story. The text can be recited as poetry, or it can be rapped or sung if the students would like to add melody or beats.

Artemis

As swift and graceful as a sparrow,
Especially skilled with a bow and arrow,
Beautiful, fierce, and fearful of nothing,
Artemis is known as the goddess of hunting.

One day, while hunting in the forest for all,
She met a handsome man nearly 70 feet tall!
Walking on water, skilled with a bow
Orion showed Artemis all the love he could show.

Together, they hunted and sped through the woods
Tracking down all the animals they could
Apollo was jealous and quickly got mad
He wanted what Orion and his sister had.

He took Artemis for target practice by the sea,
But didn't tell her what the target would be
No sorrow could match the pain she felt
When Orion left the world to be Orion's Belt.

FOLLOW-UP ACTIVITIES:

1. CREATIVE WRITING:

- Continue to work with the children on their own original poetry based on the story. (Use the word bank created earlier in the week.)

- Have older children work on writing their own version of the story with illustrations. This is best done in their individual notebook, lined on one side and blank on the other. See the Appendix for photos of this kind of notebook with sample student writing and illustrations. Or, record the student's poem in Nyansa's Year One Literature Workbook.

- Close out the story by inviting students to present the poetry, pictures, and/or other writing they have done this week.

2. CLOSING GAME SUGGESTIONS:

- Number Knockout - links and explanations of this game can be found in our Teacher's Guide book, available for purchase on our website.

- Review games - these include Latin and other review games for our literature curriculum. For example, use 3x5 cards. Put the names of the gods and goddesses on one side of the card and what they are known for on a separate 3x5 card. Throughout the weeks, you can review the gods and goddesses by matching the name of the god or goddess with what they are known for. For more ideas, see our Teacher's Guide.

Literature Group Week 8– Artemis
Day 4

See Learning Through Art

On day four, we encourage you to use the Nyansa Art Curriculum. Students will learn to build observation skills and habits of attention. They will also engage in group discussions that discuss our virtues for the week.

If you do not have the Nyansa Year One Art Curriculum, you can use the illustrations from this week's lessons. Have your students look at the illustration for 2 minutes. After the two minutes, turn over the page. Ask your student to describe the illustration back to you without looking at the picture. Then, discuss how the illustrations for this week tell the story of this week's Greek Myth through the images they observed.

Literature Group Week 9– Prometheus
Day 1
Lesson 1: Prometheus - Greek Titan

Focus Virtue: Self-discipline is being able to do the right thing even when tempted to do something else.

Focus Vice: Indiscipline is acting without considering the consequences.

Discuss the virtue and what each means. Create a new memory card for each term with its meaning and its opposite on the back of the card. More details can be found in previous weeks. Introduce the story of Artemis by allowing the students two minutes to examine her portrait. Then, turn over the portrait and ask the students to recall what they saw. Use the portrait discussion and the following facts to introduce the story:

Use the following illustrations for this week.

INTRODUCTION:

Many cultures have stories that explain where this world came from, and the Greeks were no different. The god Prometheus, they said, had made humans, given them fire, and taught them how to talk. Strictly speaking, Prometheus was not technically a god. Actually, he was a Titan, which was a type of giant that the Greek gods were said to have overthrown in order to rule on Mount Olympus. According to legend, clever Prometheus had helped Zeus overcome the other Titans. After he became king, Zeus then gave Prometheus the job of creating all the creatures on the earth. Unfortunately, creation did not go as smoothly as Prometheus had hoped.

READ:

Read the story of Prometheus (Greek Gods #9). Encourage narration activities as students listen (drawing, writing, etc).

Prometheus

In the beginning, the gods made all the plants on the earth. Then, they gave the job of creating the animals to Prometheus. Unwisely, Prometheus invited his brother Epimetheus to help him. He gave Epimetheus the job of giving each animal a way to protect and feed itself. To some, Epimetheus gave fur and claws, to others, scales and strong jaws. Epimetheus was so excited to help that he did his job carelessly. When he got to mankind, he had no gifts left to give him. Man was left naked, soft, and helpless, without warm fur or sharp claws or *anything* to protect him. When Prometheus looked over his brother's work, he felt responsible. Mankind was more godlike than the animals - it was not good that man should be so helpless. And so Prometheus gave two special gifts to mankind: first, he taught mankind how to talk, and second, he gave mankind the gift of fire.

This second gift caused a lot of issues. Prometheus didn't have any fire to give mankind. To get it, he had to steal it from Hephaestus and Athena, hidden in a hollow tube of fennel. (Fennel is a plant you can eat - it is similar to celery, but it's a lot more flavorful.) Before, the gods had occasionally given men fire, but mankind did not know how to keep the fires lit. Prometheus taught them to cover the fire with coals at night to keep the fire burning. Mankind was thrilled, and they used this fire to cook food for themselves and to forge weapons.

Zeus was furious. Prometheus had acted against his orders and had to be punished. He would not allow mankind to grow too powerful because he feared they would rise up against him, just as the gods had risen up against the Titans. Zeus ordered Hephaestus to capture Prometheus and tie him to a rock. The angry king of the gods then sent an eagle to eat Prometheus' heart. Each night, Prometheus' heart would regrow, and every morning, the eagle would return to eat it. Zeus eventually relented and allowed his heroic son, Hercules, to rescue Prometheus, but that story is for another time.

Zeus also decided to punish Epimetheus. At first, he pretended to be delighted with Prometheus' work, and he, too, promised to give a gift. Cunning Zeus made the very first woman - a beautiful bride for Epimetheus. He ordered Hephaestus to fashion her out of the ground by mixing dirt and water. Then, Aphrodite gave her grace and charm. Wise Athena taught her how to weave and put her in beautiful clothes. Clever Hermes gave her the gift of speech, but he also taught her how to lie and deceive, just as Zeus had commanded. The gods named her Pandora, which means "all gifts." As a final touch, Zeus gave her a beautiful box as a wedding present.

"Be careful not to open it," Zeus said. Then, he sent Pandora to Epimetheus as a bride.

Epimetheus was overjoyed. A present from Zeus! And such a lovely present! Now, Prometheus was much more clever than his brother. He had warned his brother that Zeus would not be happy about the fire and that under NO circumstances should he accept a present from Zeus. But Epimetheus could not help himself. He must have Pandora for his wife. And so he married her and brought her to the earth to live with him. Pandora went with him gladly, carrying her little box.

Now, Pandora was really curious about her little box. When she put her head near it, she could hear little voices. She knew that Zeus had warned her not to open it, but one thing the gods had not given Pandora was self-control. She was just so curious. She could not bear it! She must know what was inside. So one day she snuck into her room and opened the box. Immediately, all the good gifts from the gods to mankind escaped and flew back to heaven. Instead of peace and happiness, humanity would have disease, hard work, death, and war. As she saw the spirits escaping, Pandora quickly replaced the lid and managed to catch the last spirit still inside. The last spirit's name was Hope, and that spirit remained to comfort mankind.

Language Note: *Prometheus' name means "to think beforehand." His brother's name Epimetheus means 'to think afterwards." In what ways did Epimetheus not think before he acted?*

DISCUSS:

Discussion Questions:

1. Why did Prometheus give fire to mankind? What happened as a result? Was he wrong to steal from the gods?

2. Who lacked self-discipline in this story? How did they demonstrate their indiscipline?

3. In this story, why are women created? What are they like? What does this tell us about how the Greeks viewed women?

4. According to this story, why do bad things happen in the world?

5. What was the result of Pandora catching the spirit, Hope? What is hope?

6. [Christian] How does this creation story differ from the story in Genesis? What does it tell us about how the Greeks thought about their gods?

MEMORY:

Memory Sentence: Prometheus was punished by Zeus for giving fire to mankind.

FOLLOW-UP ACTIVITIES:

1. **DRESS UP**

   • Have the children act out the story. Suggested dress-up items:

pretend torch (Prometheus' fire)	flowers (Aphrodite)
crown (Zeus)	sandals with wings (Hermes)
fennel (Prometheus)	armor/shield (Athena)
fancy clothes (Pandora)	hammer (Hephaestus)
small box (Pandora)	building tools (Epithalamus)

2. **BRAINSTORM**

   • Use a full-color picture of Prometheus. Brainstorm words for the people (characters), places (setting), or things (objects) from the story. For more details, see previous lessons.

People
- Prometheus - Titan, giant, kind, generous, thief, tortured, punished, freed
- Zeus - clever, punishing, angry, judging, tormenting
- Epithalamus - undisciplined, reckless, thoughtless, disobedient, lured, tricked
- Pandora - beautiful, graceful, charming, deceitful, curious, undisciplined, sorrowful, disobedient, gifted
- Hephaestus - punishing, chaining, forming, creating
- Hermes/Aphrodite, Athena - helping, tricking, punishing

Things
- Fire - forbidding, stolen, given, cherished
- Box - forbidden, opened, full of sorrow, hopeful, gifted

Literature Group Week 9– Prometheus
Day 2

Focus Virtue: Self-discipline is being able to do the right thing even when tempted to do something else.

Focus Vice: Indiscipline is acting without considering the consequences.

DISCUSS:

- Review the virtue and vice concepts. Have children narrate back the story from the previous day.

- Review the memory sentences presented in the previous session.

FOLLOW-UP ACTIVITIES:

1. DICTATION:

- Individual or in Teams - For more information, see previous weeks.

Pre-K

- Prometheus - begins with P, N, Z, or B.

- Fire - begins with T, P, K, or F

- Box - begins with F, B, Y, or S

- Creation - begins with E, G, C, or U

Early Elementary

- Prometheus gave fire to mankind.

Later Elementary

- Prometheus gave fire to mankind. Zeus was angry, so he made Pandora as a punishment. She brought sorrow to the world.

2. CREATIVE WRITING:

- Go back to the brainstorming page with the word bank and complete that if there's still more to be done. For more information, see previous lessons.

3. CLOSING GAME SUGGESTIONS:

Number Knockout/ Review Games. See previous lessons for more information.

Literature Group Week 9- Prometheus
Day 3

REVIEW: Review the concepts for the virtues and vices. Use the memory cards created for the previous session. Ask the students to recall the memory sentence for this story.

MEMORIZE:

Introduce the poem below, which students can memorize as a way of remembering the key aspects of the story. The text can be recited as poetry, or it can be rapped or sung if the students would like to add melody or beats.

Prometheus

Technically, a Titan, different from a god,
Unarmed with a lightning bolt, trident, or rod,
Assigned to create all the creatures on Earth,
Prometheus controlled every human's birth.

He gave the gift of fire to all of mankind,
Though they acted like they had lost their minds!
Zeus was furious and punished the titan
While his brother watched from a distance, frightened.

Zeus wanted to punish Epimetheus too
He had a cunning plan and knew just what to do.
He crafted a woman named Pandora for his wife,
And filled her with the gifts to destroy human life.

One day, her curiosity was too much to contain
She opened the gift box and released a world of pain
The gods' gifts flew back to heaven, except for one to cope
The humans on earth were left with hope.

FOLLOW-UP ACTIVITIES:

1. CREATIVE WRITING:

- Continue to work with the children on their own original poetry based on the story. (Use the word bank created earlier in the week.)

- Have older children work on writing their own version of the story with illustrations. This is best done in their individual notebook, lined on one side and blank on the other. See the Appendix for photos of this kind of notebook with sample student writing and illustrations. Or, record the student's poem in Nyansa's Year One Literature Workbook.

- Close out the story by inviting students to present the poetry, pictures, and/or other writing they have done this week.

2. CLOSING GAME SUGGESTIONS:

- Number Knockout - links and explanations of this game can be found in our Teacher's Guide book, available for purchase on our website.

- Review games - these include Latin and other review games for our literature curriculum. For example, use 3x5 cards. Put the names of the gods and goddesses on one side of the card and what they are known for on a separate 3x5 card. Throughout the weeks, you can review the gods and goddesses by matching the name of the god or goddess with what they are known for. For more ideas, see our Teacher's Guide.

Literature Group Week 9– Prometheus
Day 4

See Learning Through Art

On day four, we encourage you to use the Nyansa Art Curriculum. Students will learn to build observation skills and habits of attention. They will also engage in group discussions that discuss our virtues for the week.

If you do not have the Nyansa Year One Art Curriculum, you can use the illustrations from this week's lessons. Have your students look at the illustration for 2 minutes. After the two minutes, turn over the page. Ask your student to describe the illustration back to you without looking at the picture. Then, discuss how the illustrations for this week tell the story of this week's Greek Myth through the images they observed.

Literature Group Week 10- Dionysus
Day 1
Lesson 1: Dionysus - Greek God of Plants, Wine, and Parties

Focus Virtue: Heroism is using your strength or knowledge to help and protect others.

Focus Vice: Exploitation is when you use someone's weakness to hurt them.

Discuss the virtue and what each means. Create a new memory card for each term with its meaning and its opposite on the back of the card. More details can be found in previous weeks. Introduce the story of Artemis by allowing the students two minutes to examine her portrait. Then, turn over the portrait and ask the students to recall what they saw. Use the portrait discussion and the following facts to introduce the story:

Use the following illustrations for this week.

INTRODUCTION:

Have you ever had too much sugar and run around in circles? Well, the Greeks thought that the god Dionysus loved that sort of fun. Dionysus was the Greek god of plants, wine, parties, and going crazy. His favorite animals were tigers, leopards, bulls, and dolphins. He was the god of a good kind of crazy - the kind you might feel during a really exciting ride or after lots of cake. But he was also the god of the scary kind of crazy - nightmares, madness, and angry fits. The Greeks thought that Dionysus rode a leopard, and they often drew him surrounded by wild girls and satyrs, which are half-man and half-goat creatures. Usually, they drew him with very long hair, holding a big cup and crowned with ivy. He was the son of Zeus and a human princess, and the Greeks believed that he had taught them the secret to making wine.

Read the story of Dionysus (Greek Gods #10). Encourage narration activities as students listen (drawing, writing, etc).

Dionysus

Once, Dionysus wanted to travel across the Aegean Sea between two islands, Ikaria and Naxos. A strange ship was passing by. It was covered in scales and painted to look like a sea monster with large threatening eyes painted on the front. Dionysus hailed it and asked for a ride. The sailors welcomed the handsome man dressed in purple, thinking they had found a rich prince all alone and unprotected.

Although they looked like a friendly group of merchants, in reality, they were wicked pirates! At first, Dionysus did not suspect anything. He happily curled up in the corner of the boat with a snack and a drink and relaxed. He even fell asleep. Secretly, however, the sailors changed course, planning on kidnapping the young man and selling him for a slave. One of the sailors, the pilot, warned them against this plan.

"Do you think it is brave to take advantage of a kid who is all alone and unprotected?" protested the pilot, "No! It is an evil thing to do! Let him go, or beware - the gods will judge you!"

But the other sailors mocked him and put him in chains below deck.

When the boat began to pass Naxos, Dionysus woke up. Looking out upon the sea, he saw that they had left the island of Naxos behind.

"Where are you taking me?" he demanded. "We should have turned long ago to land on Naxos!" But the sailors grinned wickedly. They jumped upon him and tied him tightly with ropes.

"You fool!" they shouted, "We are not going to Naxos! You will fetch a pretty price at the slave market. Tell us, pretty prince, if you want to avoid a slave's life, who are your parents? Maybe they would be willing to pay a ransom for you?"

Dionysus realized he was sailing with worthless men who would exploit any strangers who seemed weaker than themselves. He did not answer them but smiled a small, dangerous smile. The sailors lunged forward to grab him and drag him below decks, but when they touched him, the ropes around his wrists and ankles fell off as if the ropes had been shredded.

The pirates stopped in their tracks. Maybe there was more to this young man than met the eye. Suddenly, they saw movement behind them. Slowly but surely, thick vines were climbing up the mast, and bunches of grapes were dangling from the sails.

"Surely, this man must be a god!" they murmured in despair. They ran to grab their oars and row back to Naxos. But instead of being straight, their oars were bending and twisting, and with horror, they realized that their oars had turned into snakes! Now, the pirates started to panic. They rushed to hide below deck but stopped dead in their tracks - from below, they heard the growls of wild animals - bears, panthers, and lions! The hatch to the belly of the boat opened and out ran the pilot, followed by a ferocious bear growling and showing all its teeth.

Maddened by fear, the sailors threw themselves overboard. From the water, they looked back at Dionysus and saw that the same vines that covered their masts had formed a crown for his head. He looked down at them and laughed.

"You tried to attack and sell a defenseless young stranger, but you met a god instead," said Dionysus.

"Forgive us, oh mighty one! Oh, son of Zeus! Do not let us drown!" they cried.

"I will be merciful. From now on you will protect strangers upon the sea!" declared the god, and with a wave of his hand, the men transformed into dolphins who jumped out of the water and swam away, all except for the kind pilot whom Dionysus fished out of the sea and allowed to steer the ship back to Naxos.

Cultural Note: The Greeks thought that dolphins were particularly friendly to people. Have you ever seen dolphins bob their heads? Well, the Greeks thought this was proof that dolphins loved music and dancing. In Greek myths, both Dionysus and Aphrodite ride dolphins, and Poseidon, god of the sea, uses dolphins as messengers.

DISCUSS:

Discussion Questions:

1. Why did the sailors think they could get away with selling Dionysus as a slave? What about Dionysus did they try to exploit?

2. Did anyone in the story show heroism? What was the result?

3. Have you ever seen a person bullied by someone bigger and stronger? What happened? Did anyone stand up for the person being bullied?

4. Did Dionysus show mercy to the pirates? How does his punishment compare to some of the other gods' punishments we've seen?

5. Why is the good type of crazy that Dionysus represents (singing, dancing, being silly with friends) important? We have an expression in English: blowing off some steam. Why is it important to blow off steam?

MEMORY:

Memory Sentence: Dionysus turned the evil exploiting pirates into dolphins.

FOLLOW-UP ACTIVITIES:

1. **DRESS UP**

   • Have the children act out the story. Suggested dress-up items:

wreath of ivy large cup chairs/cutout to form boat purple cloth/scarf (Dionysus)	steering wheel (paper or cardboard for the pilot, bear ears (bear)

2. **BRAINSTORM**

   • Use a full-color picture of Dionysus. Brainstorm words for the people (characters), places (setting), or things (objects) from the story. For more details, see previous lessons.

People
- Dionysus - son of Zeus, sleepy, tied, powerful, scary, merciful, angry, avenging, strong, young-looking, handsome
- Pirates - wicked , impious, deceitful, deceptive, exploitive, cruel, frightened, crazy, transformed
- Pilot - concerned, just, kind, angry, tied, imprisoned, freed, saved

Places
- Pirate Boat - monster-like, scaled, ivy-covered, transformed

Things
- Ivy - growing, creeping, surrounding, crowning, entwining
- Ropes - secure, withered, fallen

Literature Group Week 10– Dionysus
Day 2

Focus Virtue: Heroism is using your strength or knowledge to help and protect others.

Focus Vice: Exploitation is when you use someone's weakness to hurt them.

DISCUSS:

- Review the virtue and vice concepts. Have children narrate back the story from the previous day.

- Review the memory sentences presented in the previous session.

FOLLOW-UP ACTIVITIES:

1. DICTATION:

- Individual or in Teams - For more information, see previous weeks.

Pre-K

- Dionysus - begins with A, D, Z, or B.
- Pirates - begins with S, N, K, or U
- Boat - begins with O, L, Y, or B
- Transform - begins with T, E, C, or D

Early Elementary

- Dionysus turned the pirates into dolphins.

Later Elementary

- Some pirates captured Dionysus. They wanted to sell him as a slave, but Dionysus transformed them into dolphins.

2. CREATIVE WRITING:

- Go back to the brainstorming page with the word bank and complete that if there's still more to be done. For more information, see previous lessons.

3. CLOSING GAME SUGGESTIONS:

Number Knockout/ Review Games. See previous lessons for more information.

Literature Group Week 10– Dionysus
Day 3

REVIEW: Review the concepts for the virtues and vices. Use the memory cards created for the previous session. Ask the students to recall the memory sentence for this story.

MEMORIZE:

Introduce the poem below, which students can memorize as a way of remembering the key aspects of the story. The text can be recited as poetry, or it can be rapped or sung if the students would like to add melody or beats.

The Story of Dionysus

Many years ago, in a far-off land
There lived a crazy god of wine, parties, and plants.
Taming animals from tigers to bulls,
Dionysus's cup was always full.

One day, on his travels through the sea,
He spotted a monster, could it really be?
The monster turned out to be a pirate ship,
He hoped it would aid him on his long trip.

At first, everything seemed fine
Until the sailors changed course, and things started to decline.
Just as Dionysus began to nap,
He realized that he was being kidnapped!

The clever god had many tricks up his sleeve,
He turned the oars into snakes so that he could leave.
Turning all his captors into dolphins but one,
Dionysus was free and feared no one!

FOLLOW-UP ACTIVITIES:

1. CREATIVE WRITING:

- Continue to work with the children on their own original poetry based on the story. (Use the word bank created earlier in the week.)

- Have older children work on writing their own version of the story with illustrations. This is best done in their individual notebook, lined on one side and blank on the other. See the Appendix for photos of this kind of notebook with sample student writing and illustrations. Or, record the student's poem in Nyansa's Year One Literature Workbook.

- Close out the story by inviting students to present the poetry, pictures, and/or other writing they have done this week.

2. CLOSING GAME SUGGESTIONS:

- Number Knockout - links and explanations of this game can be found in our Teacher's Guide book, available for purchase on our website.

- Review games - these include Latin and other review games for our literature curriculum. For example, use 3x5 cards. Put the names of the gods and goddesses on one side of the card and what they are known for on a separate 3x5 card. Throughout the weeks, you can review the gods and goddesses by matching the name of the god or goddess with what they are known for. For more ideas, see our Teacher's Guide.

Literature Group Week 10– Dionysus Day 4

See Learning Through Art

On day four, we encourage you to use the Nyansa Art Curriculum. Students will learn to build observation skills and habits of attention. They will also engage in group discussions that discuss our virtues for the week.

If you do not have the Nyansa Year One Art Curriculum, you can use the illustrations from this week's lessons. Have your students look at the illustration for 2 minutes. After the two minutes, turn over the page. Ask your student to describe the illustration back to you without looking at the picture. Then, discuss how the illustrations for this week tell the story of this week's Greek Myth through the images they observed.

Literature Group Week 11– Hades
Day 1
Lesson 1: Hades - Greek God of Death

Focus Virtue: Generosity is giving whatever you have to others cheerfully.

Focus Vice: Miserliness is selfishly keeping everything you have for yourself.

Discuss the virtue and what each means. Create a new memory card for each term with its meaning and its opposite on the back of the card. More details can be found in previous weeks. Introduce the story of Artemis by allowing the students two minutes to examine her portrait. Then, turn over the portrait and ask the students to recall what they saw. Use the portrait discussion and the following facts to introduce the story:

Use the following illustrations for this week.

INTRODUCTION:

The grumpiest, most solemn, gloomiest god of the Greeks was the god of death, Hades. Brother to Zeus and Poseidon, he ruled the darkest third of creation - the land of the dead, gloomy Erebus. Hades ruled that land with his beautiful wife, Persephone, whom he had stolen from her mother, the goddess Demeter. When the Greeks painted vases or sculpted statues of Hades, they imagined him as a strong man with dark hair falling on his forehead and a thick, bushy black beard. In most of the stories about him, Hades is very stern, a god to be feared, not loved. The Greeks believed that Hades had a helmet that made him invisible. They felt they never knew when death might sneak up on them!

Hades was not all bad, though. They also thought he was the god who gave them riches out of the earth - gems and jewels, gold and silver. Because of this, they called him "Plouton," which means the Lord of Riches. Believing that the god lived under the earth, they also thought that he controlled what grew out of the soil, and so they also thought Hades helped the crops to grow.

The Greeks believed that once they died, Hades would jealously guard their soul in his dark world and never allow them to see the sun again. Hades had his own three-headed dog named Cerberus, who guarded the road to his kingdom. The ferocious beast would allow souls to pass him into Erebus, but he allowed no one out. Well, almost no one. There are several famous Greek myths about people who managed to enter Erebus and come out again, but they were great heroes, like Zeus' son Hercules. Hades hated these heroes who cheated death, as you will see in this next story.

READ:

Read the story of Hades (Greek Gods #11). Encourage narration activities as students listen (drawing, writing, etc).

Hades

The god of healing and archery, Apollo, fell in love with a human princess. Her name was Coronis, and together they had a son named Asklepios. The boy inherited his father's healing abilities, and he was raised by a centaur named Chiron. The centaur was honored to have a heavenly child in his charge, and he raised him well, instructing him in the art of healing. Asklepios became so skilled at healing that some said that he had god-like powers. Without thought for himself, Asklepios spent his life healing the sick, tending to wounds, making medicine, and teaching others how to heal. He did not care about money or fame, and so he gave help to whoever asked and taught whomever he could.

Down in Erebos, Hades was frustrated. He had noticed that fewer and fewer people were coming down to his dark land. How could it be that fewer people were dying? Everyone has to die sometime, so why wasn't he seeing more traffic? Hades hated every soul who walked under the sun, and he couldn't stand being cheated, so he started asking questions. It soon came to his ears that there was a new doctor on earth who kept healing the sick and tending to the wounded so that they actually got better and lived longer. The nerve! How dare he cheat the Lord of Death? Hades sat on his dark throne, brooding on how to rid the world of Asklepios.

One day, Asklepios was called to tend to a prince named Hippolytos who lay dying from horrible injuries. As Asklepios stood over the man pondering how to treat him, a snake came into the room where he was and wove itself up his staff. He struck the snake with his stick many times until it died. Looking back at the bed, he saw that Hippolytos had died. The house rang with the cries of the family mourning for the young man they had loved. A few minutes later, a second snake wound its way into the room with some leaves in its mouth, which it put on the head of the dead snake. The dead snake then lifted its head, and the snakes left the room together! Asklepios recognized the herb. He made a powder from the leaves and then rubbed the powder on Hippolytos' chest. Breath came back into the man's body, and Hippolytos sat up in bed! Shouts of joy and surprise rang out, and word quickly spread that Asklepios could call back the dead.

When Hades heard that Asklepios was raising the dead, he was furious. This was the last straw. Hades wrote up a charge against Asklepios. He made two accusations. The first was that fewer people were dying due to Asklepios' new medicines and treatments. The second was that Asklepios was stealing souls from him by his unlawful behavior of raising the dead. The messengers of Hades rode up to Olympus and delivered the charge to the judge of heaven, almighty Zeus.

The god of heaven reviewed the charge, frowning. Zeus was fond of his own son Apollo and, therefore, was inclined to treat his grandson well. The first accusation didn't seem that bad. Certainly, a man who generously spent his life healing others should be rewarded, not punished. Then he read the second accusation. Oh dear! Are people coming back to life?! This was a very, very bad idea. If people could be brought back to life, they would not fear the gods! There would be no order, no justice, no piety! How dare Asklepios wake the dead! Mighty Zeus looked down from the heights of Mount Olympus. His keen eye spied Asklepios doing his good work of healing. With a mighty cry, Zeus threw his thunderbolt and struck Asklepios dead.

When Apollo heard that Hades had persuaded Zeus to kill his son, he was filled with fury and sorrow. With haste, he climbed Mount Olympus and strode into his father's lofty halls. With tears and threats, Apollo begged Zeus to restore his son to life, but Zeus would not. The god of heaven did feel badly for Apollo though, and allowed his son to place

Asklepios among the stars - a shining constellation for all time of a man holding a snake. In dark Erebos, Hades laughed triumphantly. Again, the dead would crowd on his shores, and his kingdom would swell. But on the earth under the sun, the people whom Asklepios had taught continued healing and teaching, and so the practice of medicine spread upon the earth.

Cultural note: Have you ever noticed the symbol on the back of an ambulance? It looks like a stick with two snakes wrapped around it. Can you guess why we use that symbol on ambulances and hospitals? That's right! It refers all the way back to Asklepios and the two snakes who helped him heal people!

DISCUSS:

Discussion Questions:

1. How did Asklepios demonstrate generosity? What did he have that he was willing to give?

2. Why did Asklepios' generosity anger Hades? What does that say about Hades' character? Is Hades a generous person?

3. Did Zeus act justly? Did Asklepios deserve to die?

4. Has someone you know ever shown you generosity? Maybe they shared something with you, or gave you some of their time, or taught you something?

5. We often associate snakes with poison and dying. What does it say about medicine that these deadly symbols are used as symbols of healing?

    1. (information if the question isn't producing answers). The Greeks thought of snakes as a symbol of resurrection due to their shedding of skin. Additionally, snake venom can sometimes be used as an anti-venom!

6. [Christian] How is Hades' view of death different from the true God's view of death?

MEMORY:

Memory Sentence: Asklepios angered Hades by generously healing the sick and injured.

FOLLOW-UP ACTIVITIES:

1.   DRESS UP

- Have the children act out the story. Suggested dress-up items:

black robe/cloth (Hades)	crown (Zeus)
staff (Asklepios)	thunderbolt (Zeus)
bandages	bow and arrows (Apollo)
jars for medicine	Pretend snakes
pillow (for Hippolytus)	

2.   BRAINSTORM

- Use a full-color picture of Hades. Brainstorm words for the people (characters), places (setting), or things (objects) from the story. For more details, see previous lessons.

People
- Hades - cold, dark, angry, vengeful, selfish, gloomy, scary, invisible
- Apollo - son of Zeus, healer, archer, father, angry, pleading, successful
- Asklepios - gifted, kind, generous, healing, compassionate, killed, skilled
- Hippolytus - injured, dead, resurrected
- Chiron - half-horse, skilled, teacher, kind, generous, honored

Places
- Erebos - dark, gloomy, cold, land of the dead

Things
- Staff - entwined, symbolic, snake-killer
- Snakes - deadly, killed, healed, leaf-bearing, teaching, symbolic
- Leaves - healing, resurrecting
- Thunderbolt - striking, deadly, punishing

Literature Group Week 11– Hades
Day 2

Focus Virtue: Generosity is giving whatever you have to others cheerfully.

Focus Vice: Miserliness is selfishly keeping everything you have for yourself.

DISCUSS:

- Review the virtue and vice concepts. Have children narrate back the story from the previous day.

- Review the memory sentences presented in the previous session.

FOLLOW-UP ACTIVITIES:

1. DICTATION:

- Individual or in Teams - For more information, see previous weeks.

Pre-K

- Asklepios - begins with E, D, A, or P
- Medicine - begins with M, O, P, or Q
- Hades - begins with T, R, L, or H
- Zeus - begins with U, K, S, or Z

NYANSA
CLASSICAL COMMUNITY
Student Dictation Sheet for Pre-K and Kindergarten

1. E D A P   3. T R L H
2. M O P Q   4. U K S Z

Early Elementary

- Zeus punished Asklepios for raising the dead.

Later Elementary

- Asklepios generously helped people who were sick and wounded. When he raised a dead person, Zeus punished him.

2. CREATIVE WRITING:

- Go back to the brainstorming page with the word bank and complete that if there's still more to be done. For more information, see previous lessons.

3. CLOSING GAME SUGGESTIONS:

Number Knockout/ Review Games. See previous lessons for more information.

Literature Group Week 11- Hades
Day 3

REVIEW: Review the concepts for the virtues and vices. Use the memory cards created for the previous session. Ask the students to recall the memory sentence for this story.

MEMORIZE:

Introduce the poem below, which students can memorize as a way of remembering the key aspects of the story. The text can be recited as poetry, or it can be rapped or sung if the students would like to add melody or beats.

Hades of the Underworld

The meanest, grumpiest god of the Greeks,
Known to be a tyrant, preying on the weak,
Snatching souls of those who took their last breath,
Hades was known as the god of death.

He ruled in the depths of the underworld,
His wife, Persephone was no more than a girl.
A surprising fact that many don't know,
Was that Hades made jewels and helped crops grow.

One day, he got word of the son of a god,
Who was healing the sick, and changing lives abroad.
He cheated death with a medicinal dose,
Hades was determined to stop Asklepios.

He charged him with bringing the dead back to life,
And presented the notion to Zeus and his wife.
Zeus was furious and had him killed in thin air,
All for starting the practice of healthcare.

FOLLOW-UP ACTIVITIES:

1. CREATIVE WRITING:

- Continue to work with the children on their own original poetry based on the story. (Use the word bank created earlier in the week.)

- Have older children work on writing their own version of the story with illustrations. This is best done in their individual notebook, lined on one side and blank on the other. See the Appendix for photos of this kind of notebook with sample student writing and illustrations. Or, record the student's poem in Nyansa's Year One Literature Workbook.

- Close out the story by inviting students to present the poetry, pictures, and/or other writing they have done this week.

2. CLOSING GAME SUGGESTIONS:

- Number Knockout - links and explanations of this game can be found in our Teacher's Guide book, available for purchase on our website.

- Review games - these include Latin and other review games for our literature curriculum. For example, use 3x5 cards. Put the names of the gods and goddesses on one side of the card and what they are known for on a separate 3x5 card. Throughout the weeks, you can review the gods and goddesses by matching the name of the god or goddess with what they are known for. For more ideas, see our Teacher's Guide.

Literature Group Week 11– Hades
Day 4

See Learning Through Art

On day four, we encourage you to use the Nyansa Art Curriculum. Students will learn to build observation skills and habits of attention. They will also engage in group discussions that discuss our virtues for the week.

If you do not have the Nyansa Year One Art Curriculum, you can use the illustrations from this week's lessons. Have your students look at the illustration for 2 minutes. After the two minutes, turn over the page. Ask your student to describe the illustration back to you without looking at the picture. Then, discuss how the illustrations for this week tell the story of this week's Greek Myth through the images they observed.

Lesson 1: Hestia - Greek Goddess of the Hearth

Focus Virtue: Hospitality is welcoming others into your home and looking to serve them.

Focus Vice: Inhospitality is being unwelcoming and rude to others in your home.

Discuss the virtue and what each means. Create a new memory card for each term with its meaning and its opposite on the back of the card. More details can be found in previous weeks. Introduce the story of Artemis by allowing the students two minutes to examine her portrait. Then, turn over the portrait and ask the students to recall what they saw. Use the portrait discussion and the following facts to introduce the story:

Use the following illustrations for this week.

INTRODUCTION:

Have you ever heard the saying, "The kitchen is the heart of the home"? There is something so welcoming about the smell of good food cooking, the warmth and coziness of the oven and stove, and the fun of getting snacks from the fridge. The Greeks associated that same feeling of coziness with their kitchens, but they didn't have fridges, electric ovens, and stoves. Instead, in the middle of the house would be a fireplace called a hearth. The women of the family would cook much of the food in this fire, and the heat would bring warmth to the whole house. In the ancient world, they did not have matches, so keeping the fires lit at all times was very important. If the fire went out, it could be very hard to relight. When they went on journeys, they would even take some of the fire from their hearths with them to start cooking fires. In this way, they brought a bit of home with them wherever they went.

In ancient times, just like today, they thought that feeding people was part of welcoming people into their homes. Cooking on the hearth was connected to showing hospitality to family, friends, and even strangers. The Greeks believed that Zeus demanded that they welcome strangers into their homes and feed them. Many Greek myths include stories of families entertaining gods and heroes, often disguised as simple travelers. The gods, they believed, would bless those who gave food and drink generously to visitors.

READ:

Read the story of Hestia (Greek Gods #12). Encourage narration activities as students listen (drawing, writing, etc).

Hestia

Hestia was the Greek goddess devoted to the hearth. She was the oldest sister of Zeus, Hera, Hades, and Poseidon, and her job was to guard the sacred fires on Mount Olympus. In art, the Greeks depicted her as a modestly dressed woman wearing a veil and carrying a kettle for boiling water and some flowers. Donkeys were her favorite animal, and so they often drew one standing next to her. There are very few stories about Hestia because the Greeks believed she never left Mount Olympus. Instead, she was content to devote her life to making a home for the other gods and goddesses. By tending to the fires, she ensured that their eternal home would be full of food, hot water, and warmth. She made their home homey. The Greeks loved Hestia and worshiped her whenever they cooked over a fire. They believed she protected the fire in their hearts and that she had taught them to build homes and fireplaces.

Hestia got the job of protecting the fire because she was a lover of peace. By all accounts, Hestia was very beautiful, and two of the other gods fell in love with her: Poseidon and Apollo. Apollo was the god of war, fierce and skilled in battle. Poseidon was the brother of Zeus, mighty and cold with his powerful trident. Gentle Hestia knew that if she chose to marry one or the other, the gods would war with each other. She could not bear to think of the horrible violence the fighting would cause, and so she came to Zeus with a special request.

"Oh, Zeus, king, and younger brother," said the quiet goddess, "please grant me this request. I ask you to allow me to never marry. I know that powerful Poseidon and gifted Apollo are both asking you for my hand in marriage, but please, please allow me to be single forever."

This request pleased Zeus. He said, "Gentle sister, you may indeed stay single. You may live here with me in my house on Mount Olympus forever. You will have the honor of guarding the fire. Every time mankind offers up a sacrifice in fire to the gods, it will come first to you, dear oldest sister."

Hestia agreed and happily took her place next to the fire. She took on a life of service to her own family, centered around keeping their home warm and full of good food.

The Greeks often talked about the gods as if they were the stars or planets, always moving past the earth across the night sky. In a way, they imagined Hestia in the very warm center of the earth, feeding the fire and offering hospitality to her own family as they passed by in the sky on their important business. Instead of warring and fighting and striving like the other gods and goddesses, gentle Hestia spent her time guarding the flame of heaven and blessing the fires of mankind below. The Greeks loved Hestia for this and believed that she took the first portion of all of their sacrifices. She was the goddess of every fire, of every sacrifice, and of every home.

Cultural Note: *Have you ever heard a campfire crackling? The Greek philosopher Aristotle said that the sound of the fire crackling was the sound of the goddess Hestia laughing!*

DISCUSS:

Discussion Questions:

1. How does Hestia demonstrate hospitality?
2. What does hospitality look like?
3. Can you think of some simple ways you can make people feel comfortable in your home? What sort of ways would Hestia suggest, do you think?
4. [Christian] How are hospitality and love connected? Can you show love by showing hospitality?
5. [Christian]Who does God want us to be hospitable to?

MEMORY:

Memory Sentence: Hestia showed hospitality to the gods by protecting the hearth.

FOLLOW-UP ACTIVITIES:

1. **DRESS UP**

   - Have the children act out the story. Suggested dress-up items:

stones to make a fireplace	bow and arrows (Apollo)
kettle	crown (Zeus)
trident (Poseidon)	veil (Hestia)

2. **BRAINSTORM**

   - Use a full-color picture of Hestia. Brainstorm words for the people (characters), places (setting), or things (objects) from the story. For more details, see previous lessons.

   People
   - Hestia - kind, gentle, contented, domestic, hospitable, peaceable, beautiful
   - Zeus - please, fair, honoring, protective
   - Apollo - waring, clever, fierce
   - Poseidon - waring, strong, powerful

   Places
   - Mount Olympus - home of the gods, welcoming, guarded, warm

   Things
   - Hearth - warm, cozy, lit, glowing, hospitable

Literature Group Week 12– Hestia
Day 2

Focus Virtue: Hospitality is welcoming others into your home and looking to serve them.

Focus Vice: Inhospitality is being unwelcoming and rude to others in your home.

DISCUSS:

- Review the virtue and vice concepts. Have children narrate back the story from the previous day.
- Review the memory sentences presented in the previous session.

FOLLOW-UP ACTIVITIES:

1. DICTATION:

- Individual or in Teams - For more information, see previous weeks.

Pre-K

- Hestia - begins with N, B, H, or L
- Zeus - begins with M, P, O, or Z
- Apollo - begins with D, R, A, or S
- Poseidon- begins with P, K, V, or G

Early Elementary

- Hestia chose to protect the hearth.

Later Elementary

- Hestia did not want to cause a war by choosing between Apollo and Poseidon. Instead, she chose to guard the hearth on Mount Olympus.

2. CREATIVE WRITING:

- Go back to the brainstorming page with the word bank and complete that if there's still more to be done. For more information, see previous lessons.

3. CLOSING GAME SUGGESTIONS:

Number Knockout/ Review Games. See previous lessons for more information.

Literature Group Week 12– Hestia
Day 3

REVIEW: Review the concepts for the virtues and vices. Use the memory cards created for the previous session. Ask the students to recall the memory sentence for this story.

MEMORIZE:

Introduce the poem below, which students can memorize as a way of remembering the key aspects of the story. The text can be recited as poetry, or it can be rapped or sung if the students would like to add melody or beats.

Hestia

As loving and nurturing as Mother Earth
Goddess Hestia was the goddess of the hearth.
Guardian of fire, tending to family, food, and love
Hestia spread warmth to the world from heaven above.

Always radiating beauty and peace,
Hestia became the darling of all of Greece
Selfless enough to maintain every fire
The hearts of the gods became filled with desire.

Poseidon and Apollo, the most powerful in the land,
Both longed for Hestia and asked for her hand
She knew that choosing only one would be the start of a war
And couldn't bear to be the reason that the world's heart tore.

She begged Zeus to let her stay single forever
So she could go on blessing the Earth and all its endeavors
She lead a life of service for the rest of her days,
And always made sure to keep the fires ablaze.

FOLLOW-UP ACTIVITIES:

1. CREATIVE WRITING:

- Continue to work with the children on their own original poetry based on the story. (Use the word bank created earlier in the week.)

- Have older children work on writing their own version of the story with illustrations. This is best done in their individual notebook, lined on one side and blank on the other. See the Appendix for photos of this kind of notebook with sample student writing and illustrations. Or, record the student's poem in Nyansa's Year One Literature Workbook.

- Close out the story by inviting students to present the poetry, pictures, and/or other writing they have done this week.

2. CLOSING GAME SUGGESTIONS:

- Number Knockout - links and explanations of this game can be found in our Teacher's Guide book, available for purchase on our website.

- Review games - these include Latin and other review games for our literature curriculum. For example, use 3x5 cards. Put the names of the gods and goddesses on one side of the card and what they are known for on a separate 3x5 card. Throughout the weeks, you can review the gods and goddesses by matching the name of the god or goddess with what they are known for. For more ideas, see our Teacher's Guide.

Literature Group Week 12– Hestia Day 4

See Learning Through Art

On day four, we encourage you to use the Nyansa Art Curriculum. Students will learn to build observation skills and habits of attention. They will also engage in group discussions that discuss our virtues for the week.

If you do not have the Nyansa Year One Art Curriculum, you can use the illustrations from this week's lessons. Have your students look at the illustration for 2 minutes. After the two minutes, turn over the page. Ask your student to describe the illustration back to you without looking at the picture. Then, discuss how the illustrations for this week tell the story of this week's Greek Myth through the images they observed.

Literature Group Week 13– Hermes
Day 1
Lesson 1: Hestia - Greek God of Messages

Focus Virtue: Industriousness is working hard and well at whatever you have to do.

Focus Vice: Laziness is doing work slowly and badly or refusing to work at all.

Discuss the virtue and what each means. Create a new memory card for each term with its meaning and its opposite on the back of the card. More details can be found in previous weeks. Introduce the story of Artemis by allowing the students two minutes to examine her portrait. Then, turn over the portrait and ask the students to recall what they saw. Use the portrait discussion and the following facts to introduce the story:

Use the following illustrations for this week.

INTRODUCTION:

All the Greek gods have their own special work and special projects, but perhaps the busiest of them all is Hermes, the son of Zeus, the messenger god. In many myths, Hermes spends his time going back and forth between gods and goddesses or between the gods and people. Usually, Hermes wears a broad traveling hat on his head and golden sandals with small wings. In his hands, he carries a staff, sometimes with twin snakes curled around it. Rams, hares (which are like large rabbits), and tortoises were special to Hermes. According to legends, when Hermes was very young, he invented the lyre (which is like a small harp) by tying strings across the empty shell of a tortoise.

Besides carrying messages, the Greeks thought that Hermes oversaw travelers, hospitality, and roads - things that had to do with going from one place to another. They figured that as a great traveler himself, Hermes would naturally care about these sorts of things. In addition to traveling, they also thought that Hermes oversaw all sorts of talking. Writing, talks of war and peace between nations, arguments between people, the ability to deceive others with words - all these things were under Hermes' care. They also believed that Hermes had invented the practice of sacrificing animals to the gods, and so they thought he was also the god of sheep and flocks. The Greeks thought of Hermes as a hard-working and clever god.

READ:

Read the story of Hermes (Greek Gods #13). Encourage narration activities as students listen (drawing, writing, etc).

Hermes

The gods often sent Hermes to carry important messages. When Zeus and Hera were married, they had a huge wedding, and they invited everyone to attend - gods and goddesses, nymphs and satyrs, birds and beasts. The couple sent Hermes to deliver the invitations. With speed and skill, Hermes found each being and delivered the invitation. Of course, it was a grand affair. The wedding of the king and queen of heaven was a special occasion, and everyone was excited to come. Well, almost everyone.

Chelone was a nymph who lived on a mountain in southern Greece in a region called Arkadia. A nymph, in case you haven't met one, is a goddess of nature, like a goddess of a river or of a flower. You might think of them a bit like fairies. Chelone lived on a bare mountain without trees or large bushes. Perhaps, living far away from her sisters of the wood and water had left her with too little to do, but whatever the reason, Chelone was lazy. She could not be bothered to do anything or go anywhere. So when busy Hermes came with her wedding invitation, she lazily dropped it on the ground, yawned, and decided she had far too much to do… like taking another nap.

The day of the wedding dawned - a day of unsurpassed glory and brightness. On lofty Mount Olympos, Zeus stood to receive his guests, his eagle perched on his broad shoulders. Next to him stood queenly Hera covered with a sweet veil and bridal robes. Bringing presents and decked in their best clothes, all of the gods, spirits, and beasts arrived. In pranced Pan, playing a sweet song on his pipes in honor of the glad couple.

Aphrodite skipped up to the couple, her arms full of flowers for the bride. Naiads, dryads, satyrs, and giants soon filled the beautiful halls, ready for the celebration. All-knowing Zeus, however, saw one place missing.

He summoned Hermes and said, "Where is that nymph Chelone?"

"I have no idea, oh King," said Hermes, "I assure you I delivered your invitation, as you commanded. If the nymph is not here, something must have gone wrong."

"Go and find out," said Zeus. Immediately, industrious Hermes obeyed. Grabbing his staff, he sped back to dry Arkadia. He walked into Chelone's house without knocking, only to find the lazy nymph sleeping in the middle of the day.

"Why are you not attending the wedding, nymph?" demanded Hermes.

"I didn't see the point," yawned Chelone, "Besides, the wedding was at the same time as my nap." She rubbed her eyes and turned over to go back to sleep. This infuriated Hermes.

"You will regret your laziness, Chelone!" shouted Hermes, "I will make your life much more difficult." Angrily, Hermes picked up the sleepy nymph and carried her down the mountain to a river. Lifting her high above his shoulders, he cast her into the river. Gasping and sputtering, the nymph started to climb out of the water, but speedy Hermes grabbed Chelone's house from the top of the hill and hurled it on top of her. Immediately, she transformed into a hard, squat animal, covered in a shell.

"As a punishment for your laziness, Chelone," said Hermes, "You will carry your house with you for the rest of your days." Feeling that he had done justice, Hermes sped back to Mount Olympus to enjoy the wedding, but Chelone struggled to reclimb her dry mountain with her hard shell of a house on her back.

Language note: *In ancient days, Arcadia was covered in tortoises, and Chelone's name means "tortoise" in Greek! What animal do you think Hermes turned Chelone into?*

DISCUSS:

Discussion Questions:

1. Why did Chelone refuse to attend the wedding?

2. Why did Chelone's actions make the gods angry?

3. How much rest is too much? How do you find a balance between being productive and taking a necessary break?

4. Who is industrious in this story? What are they like?

5. Have you ever done work that you didn't really want to do? How did you feel when the work was over?

MEMORY:

Memory Sentence: Industrious Hermes turned lazy Chelone into a tortoise.

FOLLOW-UP ACTIVITIES:

1. **DRESS UP**

   • Have the children act out the story. Suggested dress-up items:

sandals	pillow/blankets
staff	box (pretend shell)
hat (Hermes)	flowers (Aphrodite)
crown (Zeus)	pipes/flute (Pan)
veil (Heather)	

2. **BRAINSTORM**

   • Use a full-color picture of Hermes. Brainstorm words for the people (characters), places (setting), or things (objects) from the story. For more details, see previous lessons.

People
- Hermes - speedy, intelligent, industrious, clever, deceptive, hard working, reliable, musical, irritated
- Zeus - celebrating, hospitable, observant, regal, groom
- Hera - bride, beautiful, queenly
- Chelone - lazy, sleepy, rude, punished, transformed, reptilian

Places
- Arkadia - dry, treeless, bare, rocky
- Mount Olympus - heavenly, bright, shining, lofty, decorated

Things
- Invitations - sent, received, honoring, ignored

Literature Group Week 13– Hermes
Day 2

Focus Virtue: Industriousness is working hard and well at whatever you have to do.

Focus Vice: Laziness is doing work slowly and badly or refusing to work at all.

DISCUSS:

- Review the virtue and vice concepts. Have children narrate back the story from the previous day.
- Review the memory sentences presented in the previous session.

FOLLOW-UP ACTIVITIES:

1. DICTATION:

- Individual or in Teams - For more information, see previous weeks.

Pre-K

- Hermes begins with N, O, H, or P
- Tortoise begins with D, S, T, or U
- Wedding begins with W, L, R, or Q
- Lazy begins with E, I, N, or L

Early Elementary

- Hermes turned Chelone into a tortoise.

Later Elementary

- Industrious Hermes delivered the wedding invitations.
- Lazy Chelone refused to come. Hermes turned her into a tortoise.

2. CREATIVE WRITING:

- Go back to the brainstorming page with the word bank and complete that if there's still more to be done. For more information, see previous lessons.

3. CLOSING GAME SUGGESTIONS:

Number Knockout/ Review Games. See previous lessons for more information.

Literature Group Week 13– Hermes
Day 3

REVIEW: Review the concepts for the virtues and vices. Use the memory cards created for the previous session. Ask the students to recall the memory sentence for this story.

MEMORIZE:

Introduce the poem below, which students can memorize as a way of remembering the key aspects of the story. The text can be recited as poetry, or it can be rapped or sung if the students would like to add melody or beats.

Hermes

Messenger of the gods and son of the king,
Hermes controlled the travel of everyone and everything
Clever and hardworking, to say the least
Hermes was a messenger for every man, woman, and beast.

On the day Zeus and Hera were set to be married
Wedding invitations were all that Zeus carried
He delivered one to to mountain nymph Chelone
Who was extra lazy and always alone.

She threw away the invitation, careless as ever,
Letting it fly through the wind as light as a feather
On the day of the wedding, filled with celebration and gleam
Chelone the nymph, was nowhere to be seen.

Hermes sped to her home to use his words to confront her
But resulted in methods a little bit rougher
He threw her in the water and turned her into a shellfish!
She'd carry her home on her back forever, no matter how hard she wished.

FOLLOW-UP ACTIVITIES:

1. CREATIVE WRITING:

- Continue to work with the children on their own original poetry based on the story. (Use the word bank created earlier in the week.)

- Have older children work on writing their own version of the story with illustrations. This is best done in their individual notebook, lined on one side and blank on the other. See the Appendix for photos of this kind of notebook with sample student writing and illustrations. Or, record the student's poem in Nyansa's Year One Literature Workbook.

- Close out the story by inviting students to present the poetry, pictures, and/or other writing they have done this week.

2. CLOSING GAME SUGGESTIONS:

- Number Knockout - links and explanations of this game can be found in our Teacher's Guide book, available for purchase on our website.

- Review games - these include Latin and other review games for our literature curriculum. For example, use 3x5 cards. Put the names of the gods and goddesses on one side of the card and what they are known for on a separate 3x5 card. Throughout the weeks, you can review the gods and goddesses by matching the name of the god or goddess with what they are known for. For more ideas, see our Teacher's Guide.

Literature Group Week 13– Hermes Day 4

See Learning Through Art

On day four, we encourage you to use the Nyansa Art Curriculum. Students will learn to build observation skills and habits of attention. They will also engage in group discussions that discuss our virtues for the week.

If you do not have the Nyansa Year One Art Curriculum, you can use the illustrations from this week's lessons. Have your students look at the illustration for 2 minutes. After the two minutes, turn over the page. Ask your student to describe the illustration back to you without looking at the picture. Then, discuss how the illustrations for this week tell the story of this week's Greek Myth through the images they observed.

Literature Group Week 14- Eros
Day 1
Lesson 1: Eros - Greek God of Love

Focus Virtue: Contentment is being happy with what you have.

Focus Vice: Envy is wanting what others have so much that you wish them harm.

Discuss the virtue and what each means. Create a new memory card for each term with its meaning and its opposite on the back of the card. More details can be found in previous weeks. Introduce the story of Artemis by allowing the students two minutes to examine her portrait. Then, turn over the portrait and ask the students to recall what they saw. Use the portrait discussion and the following facts to introduce the story:

Use the following illustrations for this week.

INTRODUCTION:

Most people enjoy love stories, and the Greeks were no different. In fact, they had a god whose main job was to make people fall in love. His name was Eros, and he was the son of Aphrodite, the goddess of love and beauty. Sometimes, the Greeks drew Eros as a plump baby, and other times as a young man, but in all his pictures, he's handsome with curly hair and wings and armed with a golden bow and arrows. According to the myths, Eros would shoot people with his arrows to make them fall in love. Often, this romantic love would convince people to make unwise decisions, and so the Greeks thought of Eros as a mischief-maker. The myth you are about to read tells the story of how Eros got married.

Read the story of Eros (Greek Gods #14). Encourage narration activities as students listen (drawing, writing, etc).

Eros

A king and queen had three daughters. They were all lovely, but the youngest, named Psyche, was so beautiful that people said she equaled Aphrodite. Instead of worshiping at Aphrodite's altars, people flocked in droves to get a glimpse of Princess Psyche. Aphrodite was furious. How dare people worship a human girl instead of her? Filled with envy, the goddess called her son Eros to her.

"My son," she said, "there is a wretched human girl who is stealing away my worship. I want you to go and shoot your arrows at her. Make her fall in love with the ugliest, meanest, dirtiest man on the earth."

Eros went to see this Psyche who was making his mother so envious. When he saw her walking gracefully through the street, he fell in love with her immediately and decided to make her his bride.

Meanwhile, Psyche's father, worried that his daughter's beauty would turn the gods against him, went to the shrine of Apollo for advice. Apollo told him that as punishment for the girl's beauty, she must marry a monster in the mountains. The king was very sad, but he also feared the gods, so he put a wedding dress on his daughter and left her crying in the mountains. As she wept into the grass, Eros sent a sweet wind, called a Zephyr, to lead her gently across the craggy cliffs and grassy meadows into a pleasant valley. There, she was astonished to see a golden house with shining pillars and marble floors. Unseen voices welcomed her to the house, and invisible hands brought her food and drink.

When it was dark outside, Eros came to the house. The house was dark, and she could not see him, but his voice was beautiful. He didn't sound like a monster. Eros spoke so gently to her that she soon stopped being afraid. But before the morning light struck their lofty house, Eros slipped out. As he did, he firmly warned his wife that she must not try to see him or discover his true identity, or she would be lost to him forever. And so Psyche spent her days in the beautiful house all alone, waiting for her husband to visit after dark. Days stretched into months, and beautiful, gentle Psyche enjoyed her life in the wild mountains.

Psyche's sisters missed her terribly, and they journeyed into the mountains in hopes of finding any sign of her. Eros saw them coming and warned his wife.

"Beloved," he said, "Your sisters are looking for you in the mountains. Do not try to see them, for if you do, Fate has declared that you will suffer."

But Psyche missed the friendship of other humans, and she begged Eros to allow her a visit. Eros could not bear to see his dear wife in tears, so he agreed, and the Zephyr brought Psyche's sisters to her mountain home.

Running out the door, Psyche greeted her sisters with great joy and brought them into her house. When they saw that invisible servants brought food to their sister and that invisible hands played sweet music upon her command, they realized that their sister was not married to some mountain shepherd but to a god! Instead of being happy for their sister, their hearts are filled with envy and greed. If they couldn't be married to immortal gods, neither could their little sister. Pretending to congratulate her, they asked Psyche what her husband was like. At first, Psyche tried to change the subject, but eventually, she admitted she had never seen him. They pretended to be happy for Psyche and congratulated her on her wonderful home. No sooner had the door closed than the sisters started plotting to ruin their sister.

The next day, the evil sisters scratched their own faces, tore their clothes, and showed up crying at Psyche's door.

"Oh sister," they cried, "We were so worried when you said you had never seen your husband, so we hid in thorn bushes all night to see what sort of creature would come to you. You are married to a horrible snakey monster. You must kill it! Sneak a lamp into your room tonight, and when he's asleep, kill him, and then we will bring you home with us!"

Poor sweet Psyche was filled with so much terror that she agreed to do as her sisters had said. That night, she hid a lamp under her bed. When she heard the regular breathing of her husband sleeping deeply, she lifted up the lamp to look at him. No monster lay there but a handsome god! As she bent over him, some burning wax fell from her lamp upon his perfect shoulder. Shocked by the pain, Eros jumped up and saw her standing there. He flew away, furious she had broken his trust.

For weeks, the girl wandered in the mountains looking for Eros, but instead of finding her dear husband, she found his angry mother, Aphrodite. Psyche knew she was guilty of betraying Eros, and so she threw herself at the goddess' feet and begged for mercy. The vengeful goddess gave Psyche horribly difficult jobs to do, but the sweet girl carried them out without complaining, even though Aphrodite continued to hide her from Eros.

After a time, the other gods saw her patient spirit and felt compassion for her, and Zeus told Eros where he could find his suffering bride. Eros still really loved her, and he brought her up to Mount Olympus. There, Zeus turned Psyche into an immortal goddess. The gods threw a grand wedding party for the couple. United in love and immortality, Eros and Psyche lived happily ever after.

Cultural Note: You might have heard of Eros by his other name, Cupid. Around Valentine's Day, you often see pictures of Cupid with his bow and arrows on cards or in shop windows.

DISCUSS:

Discussion Questions:

1. Which characters in this story demonstrate envy? Was their envy justified? How does their envy change their behavior?
2. Are any characters content with what they have?
3. Have you ever felt envious of another person? How did you respond?
4. [Christian] How does the Bible tell us we can become more content?

MEMORY:

Memory Sentence: Industrious Hermes turned lazy Chelone into a tortoise.

FOLLOW-UP ACTIVITIES:

1. **DRESS UP**

    • Have the children act out the story. Suggested dress-up items:

toy bow and arrow	cups/plates
wings (Eros)	candle/lamp
tiara (Psyche)	pillow (Eros)
flower garland (Aphrodite)	

2. **BRAINSTORM**

- Use a full-color picture of Eros. Brainstorm words for the people (characters), places (setting), or things (objects) from the story. For more details, see previous lessons.

People

- Eros - mischievous, handsome, in love, sleeping, burned, married, happy, compassionate
- Psyche - sweet, beautiful, content, gracious, hospitable, deceived, distrustful, miserable, saved, married, happy
- Aphrodite - beautiful, envious, angry, spiteful, cruel
- Psyche's sister - envious, deceitful, mean, jealous, lying

Places

- Zephyr - windy, sweet, gentle, leading

Things

- Lamp - hidden, lit, revealed, dripping

Literature Group Week 14– Eros
Day 2

Focus Virtue: Contentment is being happy with what you have.

Focus Vice: Envy is wanting what others have so much that you wish them harm.

DISCUSS:

- Review the virtue and vice concepts. Have children narrate back the story from the previous day.
- Review the memory sentences presented in the previous session.

FOLLOW-UP ACTIVITIES:

1. DICTATION:

- Individual or in Teams - For more information, see previous weeks.

Pre-K

- Aphrodite - begins with A, N, U, or C.
- Zephyr - begins with T, P, K, or Z
- Marriage - begins with N, L, Y, or S
- Lamp - begins with R, G, L, or D

Early Elementary

- Eros married Psyche in secret.

Later Elementary

- Eros married Psyche, but she didn't know who he was. Her sisters tricked her into spying on Eros.

2. CREATIVE WRITING:

- Go back to the brainstorming page with the word bank and complete that if there's still more to be done. For more information, see previous lessons.

3. CLOSING GAME SUGGESTIONS:

Number Knockout/ Review Games. See previous lessons for more information.

Literature Group Week 14– Eros
Day 3

REVIEW: Review the concepts for the virtues and vices. Use the memory cards created for the previous session. Ask the students to recall the memory sentence for this story.

MEMORIZE:

Introduce the poem below, which students can memorize as a way of remembering the key aspects of the story. The text can be recited as poetry, or it can be rapped or sung if the students would like to add melody or beats.

Eros

Known for causing the gods to fall in love,
Curly-haired and handsome, with wings to fly above,
Rumored to cause trouble in his mischievous stance,
Eros was the god of marriage and romance.

One day his mother Aphrodite was angry and distraught
At a human girl named Pysche whom she could have fought
Jealous of her beauty, she sent Eros to shoot,
But he had fallen into love that he could not refute.

He visited Psyche in secret, sneaking through the dark
And warned her not to leave a trace, sound, or mark
Soon, her sisters came to see her and instantly boiled with hate
Jealous that a handsome godly husband would not be their fate.

They convinced her to try to kill him, and she nearly did as told
Until she saw his true form, such glory to behold
She worked long and hard to win him back and overcome such a disaster
Until they married in such godly glamor, living happily ever after.

FOLLOW-UP ACTIVITIES:

1. CREATIVE WRITING:

- Continue to work with the children on their own original poetry based on the story. (Use the word bank created earlier in the week.)

- Have older children work on writing their own version of the story with illustrations. This is best done in their individual notebook, lined on one side and blank on the other. See the Appendix for photos of this kind of notebook with sample student writing and illustrations. Or, record the student's poem in Nyansa's Year One Literature Workbook.

- Close out the story by inviting students to present the poetry, pictures, and/or other writing they have done this week.

2. CLOSING GAME SUGGESTIONS:

- Number Knockout - links and explanations of this game can be found in our Teacher's Guide book, available for purchase on our website.

- Review games - these include Latin and other review games for our literature curriculum. For example, use 3x5 cards. Put the names of the gods and goddesses on one side of the card and what they are known for on a separate 3x5 card. Throughout the weeks, you can review the gods and goddesses by matching the name of the god or goddess with what they are known for. For more ideas, see our Teacher's Guide.

Literature Group Week 14– Eros
Day 4

See Learning Through Art

On day four, we encourage you to use the Nyansa Art Curriculum. Students will learn to build observation skills and habits of attention. They will also engage in group discussions that discuss our virtues for the week.

If you do not have the Nyansa Year One Art Curriculum, you can use the illustrations from this week's lessons. Have your students look at the illustration for 2 minutes. After the two minutes, turn over the page. Ask your student to describe the illustration back to you without looking at the picture. Then, discuss how the illustrations for this week tell the story of this week's Greek Myth through the images they observed.

Literature Group Week 15– Poseidon
Day 1
Lesson 1: Poseidon - Greek God of the Sea

Focus Virtue: Trustworthiness is being honest and keeping your word.

Focus Vice: Untrustworthiness is telling lies, acting sneakily, or breaking promises.

Discuss the virtue and what each means. Create a new memory card for each term with its meaning and its opposite on the back of the card. More details can be found in previous weeks. Introduce the story of Artemis by allowing the students two minutes to examine her portrait. Then, turn over the portrait and ask the students to recall what they saw. Use the portrait discussion and the following facts to introduce the story:

Use the following illustrations for this week.

INTRODUCTION:

Poseidon, the King of the Sea, was unpredictable, changing all the time from happy to angry, from calm to crashing, just like the sea he ruled. Usually, the Greeks painted Poseidon as a powerful man with a black bushy beard, riding a chariot pulled by hippocampi, which are horse-like creatures with fishtails. In his hands, he carried a trident, which is a spear with three tips that Greek fishermen used. With his trident, Poseidon could call up storms, shatter boulders, and destroy ships. Sailors would pray to Poseidon for safe voyages, and several myths tell of famous heroes struggling at sea because they angered the watery god. The Greeks also believed that Poseidon could shake the world from below and cause earthquakes or floods.

Read the story of Poseidon (Greek Gods #15). Encourage narration activities as students listen (drawing, writing, etc).

Poseidon

Once, Poseidon revolted against Zeus. After Zeus conquered his brother, he punished him by making him work for a mortal king for payment. He sent him to build the walls of the great city, Troy, for King Laomedon. In exchange, King Laomedon promised to give Poseidon every bull born among his flock that year. But the king was a greedy, miserly man, and he could not bear to give the payment he had promised, so when Poseidon came for his wages, he refused to pay him and commanded him to leave his lands.

Insulted and furious, the god vowed revenge. Poseidon sent a special sea monster to attack Troy - a water dragon with a snake-like tail miles long and three rows of razor-sharp teeth! When the tide came in, the monster would strike, carrying off the people who lived around the city. The people of Troy became desperate. They sent a party to ask the Oracle of Delphi what they should do to rid themselves of the horrible monster. The oracle replied that they must willingly sacrifice their daughters from time to time, and then the monster would leave them alone. Because Laomedon had broken his promise to Posiedon and acted selfishly, their daughters must die.

From then on, every few weeks, the people would cast lots to decide whose daughter would be sacrificed. Eventually, the lot fell to the king's own sweet daughter. And so the king took his daughter Hesione down to the cliffs outside of Troy and chained her to the rocks. As his daughter wept in terror, the king felt sorry he had greedily cheated Poseidon, and the king promised that if anyone could kill the monster and free his daughter, he would give them his most precious possession - his twelve immortal horses, which had been a gift to him from Zeus himself!

Now, it just so happened that the hero of heroes, the son of Zeus, Hercules himself, was journeying along that way just at that time. As he passed the craggy cliffs, he heard a girl crying out with terror. Hercules and his traveling companion, brave Telamon, walked towards the edge and looked down. There, they saw Hesione weeping and struggling to free herself from the chains.

"Beautiful maiden," called Hercules, "Why are you chained to this cliff?"

Hesione looked up hopefully. She saw mighty Hercules and explained her sad situation.

"A sea monster, you say?" replied Hercules with a grin. "Well, that sounds like fun!" And he jumped down and freed the girl. Telamon helped her scramble up the slippery rocks, and she stood behind him. Hercules, however, remained on the cliff, awaiting the monster.

Down in the depths of the sea, seething Poseidon gave the signal with his mighty trident and sent his dreadful monster yet again to ravage the shores of Troy. Now came the slithering monster, weaving in and out of the waves. From atop the walls of Troy, it looked as if new islands had appeared all over the sea, but the men on watch knew it was the endless coils of the monster's body. On top of the cliff, Hesione screamed in terror, but down below, Hercules pulled his lion skin cloak a little closer and readied his mighty club for battle.

Up came the massive head out of the sea, dripping and stinking, with huge empty eyes and massive sharp yellow teeth. With a prayer for protection to his father Zeus, Hercules brought his mighty club down over and over and over again on the monster's neck. Surprised to find a god-like warrior on the cliff instead of a young girl, the monster drew back in surprise. Hercules seized the moment. He put several arrows in his bow and let them fly at the deadly dragon. The stinging arrows pierced the dragon's eyes and mouth, and it screamed out in pain. With a sad cry, it sank below the water and sank away from the shores of Troy.

From the city walls, shouts of joy filled the air! But one man was not happy. King Laomedon realized that Hercules would expect payment, and he did not want to honor his promise. Hercules and Telamon brought Hesione back to Troy, and Hercules demanded the immortal horses.

"I, um, I won't give them to you," stammered Laomedon, "You've done a brave thing, and you deserve a reward. Why don't you marry my daughter? That'd be enough reward, eh?"

Hesione hid her face in shame and sorrow. Here, this brave man had rescued her from a horrible death, a situation caused by her father's dishonesty, and he could not even keep his promise to her rescuer.

Hercules smiled a grim smile and replied, "Hand over the horses, or I'll take them by force."

"Try if you can!" Laomedon replied sullenly.

"Then I will return with friends, and I will take your city," vowed Hercules. Then he turned to Hesione.

"Sweet maiden," he said gently, "None of this is your fault. What would you like? I can leave you here with your family to await the coming war, or I can take you with us. My friend Talamon has fallen in love with you and would marry you if you agree."

"I will go with you, good sir!" she replied, and she went and stood near Talamon.

Some time later, Hercules did return with warriors, and he took Troy easily. As his own prize, he took the twelve white immortal horses, but Hesione lived as Talamon's wife happily ever after. And so Poseidon's revenge was complete - Laomedon lost his kingdom, his horses, his people, and his daughter.

DISCUSS:

Discussion Questions:

1. Who acted in an untrustworthy manner in this story? How were they untrustworthy? Was anyone in this story trustworthy? How so?
2. Why was Hesione ashamed of her father?
3. Was Poseidon's way of punishing Troy and Laomedon just? Why or why not?
4. Why do you think Hercules was willing to battle the monster?
5. Have you ever broken a promise to someone? Did you get a chance to make it right?

MEMORY:

Memory Sentence: Poseidon punished Laomedon for breaking his promise.

FOLLOW-UP ACTIVITIES:

1.   DRESS UP

   • Have the children act out the story. Suggested dress-up items:

trident	club (Hercules)
blankets/chairs (to build walls of Troy	tan robe (Hercules' lion skin)
tiara (Hesione)	shimmery fabric (cover sea dragon)
crown (Laomedon)	bow/arrows

2.   BRAINSTORM

   • Use a full-color picture of Poseidon. Brainstorm words for the people (characters), places (setting), or things (objects) from the story. For more details, see previous lessons.

People
   • Poseidon - changeable, rebelling, beaten, punished, unpaid, angry, vengeful, punishing
   • Laomedon - untrustworthy, greedy, lying, promise-breaking, foolish, punished, selfish, afraid
   • Hesione - afraid, sacrificed, bound, chained, abandoned, rescued, protected, married, innocent
   • Hercules - brave, conquering, heroic, saving, strong, god-like, powerful, resolute

Things
   • Sea Dragon - dangerous, scaly, horrible, dripping, fierce, sharp-toothed, beaten, defeated
   • Twelve Immortal Horses - gifted, prized, valuable, beautiful, glorious, offered, kept, won
   • Walls of Troy - built, strong, impregnable, mighty, towering

Literature Group Week 15– Poseidon
Day 2

Focus Virtue: Trustworthiness is being honest and keeping your word.

Focus Vice: Untrustworthiness is telling lies, acting sneakily, or breaking promises.

DISCUSS:

- Review the virtue and vice concepts. Have children narrate back the story from the previous day.
- Review the memory sentences presented in the previous session.

FOLLOW-UP ACTIVITIES:

1. DICTATION:

- Individual or in Teams - For more information, see previous weeks.

Pre-K

- Poseidon - begins with A, N, Z, or P
- Hercules - begins with T, H, K, or R
- Dragon - begins with O, L, D, or S
- Troy - begins with E, T, C, or M

Early Elementary

- Poseidon punished Troy with a sea dragon.

Later Elementary

- Poseidon sent a sea dragon to punish Troy. Hercules fought the monster and won. The king refused to give Hercules the reward.

2. CREATIVE WRITING:

- Go back to the brainstorming page with the word bank and complete that if there's still more to be done. For more information, see previous lessons.

3. CLOSING GAME SUGGESTIONS:

Number Knockout/ Review Games. See previous lessons for more information.

Literature Group Week 15– Poseidon
Day 3

REVIEW: Review the concepts for the virtues and vices. Use the memory cards created for the previous session. Ask the students to recall the memory sentence for this story.

MEMORIZE:

Introduce the poem below, which students can memorize as a way of remembering the key aspects of the story. The text can be recited as poetry, or it can be rapped or sung if the students would like to add melody or beats.

Poseidon

Keeper of the ocean, king of the sea,
A god much stronger than you and me,
Lead by a chariot armed with a trident,
The guardian of the water was named Poseidon.

One day, with Zeus, Poseidon revolted
But with the strength of lightning, Zeus bolted
As punishment for his disrespect,
He was sentenced to work, surrounded by neglect.

King Laomedon ordered him to build the walls of Troy,
Little did he know, it was only a ploy.
The king refused to pay him back
So Poseidon decided to lead a ruthless attack!

He sent a sea monster to the human world,
And demanded they sacrifice every young girl.
Hercules saved the city, the king was resentful
He lost everything he loved, Poseidon's revenge was successful.

FOLLOW-UP ACTIVITIES:

1. CREATIVE WRITING:

- Continue to work with the children on their own original poetry based on the story. (Use the word bank created earlier in the week.)

- Have older children work on writing their own version of the story with illustrations. This is best done in their individual notebook, lined on one side and blank on the other. See the Appendix for photos of this kind of notebook with sample student writing and illustrations. Or, record the student's poem in Nyansa's Year One Literature Workbook.

- Close out the story by inviting students to present the poetry, pictures, and/or other writing they have done this week.

2. CLOSING GAME SUGGESTIONS:

- Number Knockout - links and explanations of this game can be found in our Teacher's Guide book, available for purchase on our website.

- Review games - these include Latin and other review games for our literature curriculum. For example, use 3x5 cards. Put the names of the gods and goddesses on one side of the card and what they are known for on a separate 3x5 card. Throughout the weeks, you can review the gods and goddesses by matching the name of the god or goddess with what they are known for. For more ideas, see our Teacher's Guide.

Literature Group Week 15– Poseidon Day 4

See Learning Through Art

On day four, we encourage you to use the Nyansa Art Curriculum. Students will learn to build observation skills and habits of attention. They will also engage in group discussions that discuss our virtues for the week.

If you do not have the Nyansa Year One Art Curriculum, you can use the illustrations from this week's lessons. Have your students look at the illustration for 2 minutes. After the two minutes, turn over the page. Ask your student to describe the illustration back to you without looking at the picture. Then, discuss how the illustrations for this week tell the story of this week's Greek Myth through the images they observed.

Literature Group Week 16– Helios
Day 1
Lesson 1: Helios - Greek God of the Sun

Focus Virtue: Gentleness is being tender and kind with your actions and words.

Focus Vice: Harshness is treating others with cruelty or severity.

Discuss the virtue and what each means. Create a new memory card for each term with its meaning and its opposite on the back of the card. More details can be found in previous weeks. Introduce the story of Artemis by allowing the students two minutes to examine her portrait. Then, turn over the portrait and ask the students to recall what they saw. Use the portrait discussion and the following facts to introduce the story:

Use the following illustrations for this week.

INTRODUCTION:

Helios was the Greek god of the sun. Properly speaking, he was a Titan god, meaning that he was descended from the gods of heaven and earth. Titans came before the Olympian gods (like Zeus and Poseidon), but they were not necessarily more powerful. In the case of Helios, his parents were the gods of light and of sight, Hyperion and Theia. Helios's two jobs were shining on the earth and making sure people kept their oaths. The Greeks believed that Helios could see everything that happened on the earth; if you made a promise and broke it, he would know. Several Greek myths relate how Helios caught gods or mortals behaving badly and made sure they were punished. According to the Greeks, Helios lived in a golden palace above the ocean. Each morning, he would ride across the sky in his chariot, bringing light to the world. Four winged horses pulled his chariot. In art, the Greeks drew

Helios as a handsome man with shafts of light shining out in a circle from his head, which are called an "aureole." Some of his children included the goddesses of hours and the goddesses of seasons.

One of the other sky gods was named Boreas. He was the god of the north wind - an icy cold god, the father of snow. His brother winds were named Zepherus - the sweet west wind, Notus, the rainy south wind, and Euros, the east wind of fall breezes who lived near Helios. Of the wind gods, Boreas was the strongest and toughest. Perhaps being stronger than his brothers went to his head. Bitter and proud, he became convinced that he could do anything. After all, what could be more powerful than icy winds that blew people into their houses, huddling near fires for warmth?

READ:

Read the story of Helios (Greek Gods #16). Encourage narration activities as students listen (drawing, writing, etc).

Helios

One day, Boreas was racing through the sky when he passed Helios in his chariot, making his daily voyage across the sky.

"Oh dear!" Boreas said, with pretend politeness, "I almost bumped into you! I'd hate to knock you off your course. I can only imagine the complaints Zeus would get if you were not there to warm people after I'd frozen them solid! Haha!"

"You think you could knock me off my course?" asked Helios, with a small smile.

"Come now," replied Boreas, blowing some clouds away, "Your rays are beautiful and charming, but no one can stand against the force of my wind!"

"So you think you're stronger?" said Helios, grinning broadly this time.

"Yes, of course, I am!" replied Boreas. Helios did not answer for a minute. He looked down upon the earth, and his all-seeing eye saw a worn-out traveler walking along a mountain trail.

"Boreas, do you see that man walking along the mountain path?" asked Helios.

It took Boreas a few minutes to find him, but when he saw him, he said, "Yes, I do! What about him?"

"Who do you think he would choose as the stronger one? You or me?" asked Helios.

"Me, of course! Why, I could blow the clothes right off that poor lonely man!" boasted Helios. Helios chuckled.

"Alright! Let's make that the contest then. Whoever can get the man to take off his clothes first wins."

"You're on!" said Boreas enthusiastically. Boreas gathered himself together, ready to blow the man to pieces.

"Aren't you going to try?" asked Boreas, looking up at Helios, who sat quietly in his chariot.

"You go first!" said Helios politely, "I will wait until you're finished."

"Then you won't even get to try! I'll be done with this challenge in a minute!" sneered Boreas.

Then Boreas gathered all his might and blew and blew and blew. The poor man walking along the mountain ridge shuddered and hurried along. With a crash of his mighty hands, Boreas dropped snow and icy rain on the man, but the confused mortal just pulled his cloak tighter around him and hung on for dear life. Frustrated, Boreas tried a new tactic. Instead of blowing constantly, he stopped and waited for a minute, and then surprised the man with a sudden blast. This only frightened the poor man, and he searched for a grove of trees to hide among. Almost frozen to death, the man huddled for warmth amongst the roots of tall trees, shivering and praying for the wind to cease. The harsher Boreas blew, the tighter the man held onto his clothes. Eventually, Boreas became tired.

"Well, I've had it!" puffed Boreas. "Clothes are harder to blow off than I thought. You try!" Embarrassed and tired, Boreas threw himself down and closed his eyes for a rest.

"You tried very hard. No one could accuse you of not trying your hardest!" said Helios kindly, "But we shall see if my way is any better."

Helios looked down at the man and very, very gently shone his rays upon the poor, cold, huddled man (who was having a much worse day than he'd expected). Feeling the soft warmth, the man raised his head, and the cold drawn lines on his face relaxed into a soft smile. He stopped huddling against the trees, stood up, and started on his way again. Helios kept shining his light and warmth down on the man, not so strongly as to hurt him, but softly, like the sweet early days of summer. The man began to smile and turn his face up to enjoy the gentle rays. As he walked, he began to get hot. The man took off his cloak and slung it over his arm. Smiling, Helios shone just a little bit more brightly. Soon, a touch of sweat appeared on the man's brow, and he began to fan himself and look for a drink of water. Just then, the man passed a gently flowing spring. Feeling that a break was well deserved after his trying morning, the man stopped. The water looked cool and inviting. He stripped off his clothes and jumped into the water for a refreshing swim.

"I've won!" shouted Helios. Boreas woke up with a start.

"What?! How?" he said. Then he looked at the man bobbing happily in the water, his clothes in a pile on the shore. "HOW did you get him to do that?"

"Gentleness is better than harshness, my friend, and persuading someone to do something is better than forcing them. Remember that!" replied Helios, and he continued on his journey through the bright blue sky, bringing light and warmth to the sweet green earth.

DISCUSS:

Discussion Questions:

1. Who was harsh in this story? Did their harshness help them accomplish their goals?
2. Who was gentle? Did they succeed any better? Why?
3. Who worked harder in this story - Helios or Boreas? Did their hard work pay off?
4. Have you ever tried to get someone to do something for you? Did you try harshness or gentleness? Did you succeed?

MEMORY:

Memory Sentence: Gentle Helios won the contest with Boreas.

FOLLOW-UP ACTIVITIES:

1. **DRESS UP**

   • Have the children act out the story. Suggested dress-up items:

cloak/staff (traveler)	cotton balls (snow)
halo (Helios)	blue streams (wind)
dark cloak (Boreas)	

2. **BRAINSTORM**

   • Use the full-color picture of Helios. Brainstorm words for the people (characters), places (setting), or things (objects) from the story. For more details, see previous lessons.

   People
   - Helios - gentle, warm, bright, persuasive, calm, thoughtful, smiling
   - Boreas - brash, cold, harsh, proud, angry, tired, worn out
   - Traveler - tired, journeying, blown, swept, shivering, cowering, hiding, warmed, caressed, cheered, hot, refreshed

   Places
   - Mountain - breezy, cold, exposed

   Things
   - Chariot - bright, shining, steady, horse drawn
   - Stream - cold, inviting, refreshing, gentle

Literature Group Week 16– Helios
Day 2

Focus Virtue: Gentleness is being tender and kind with your actions and words.

Focus Vice: Harshness is treating others with cruelty or severity.

DISCUSS:

- Review the virtue and vice concepts. Have children narrate back the story from the previous day.
- Review the memory sentences presented in the previous session.

FOLLOW-UP ACTIVITIES:

1. DICTATION:

- Individual or in Teams - For more information, see previous weeks.

Pre-K

- Helios - begins with A, N, H, or C.
- Boreas - begins with B, P, K, or Z
- Sun - begins with N, L, Y, or S
- Wind - begins with R, G, W, or E

Early Elementary

- Boreas challenged Helios to a contest.

Later Elementary

- Boreas and Helios had a contest to see who was stronger. Boreas tried to blow a man's clothes off.
- Helios shone gently on the man. The man decided to go swimming. Helios won the contest.

2. CREATIVE WRITING:

- Go back to the brainstorming page with the word bank and complete that if there's still more to be done. For more information, see previous lessons.

3. CLOSING GAME SUGGESTIONS:

Number Knockout/ Review Games. See previous lessons for more information.

Literature Group Week 16 – Helios
Day 3

REVIEW: Review the concepts for the virtues and vices. Use the memory cards created for the previous session. Ask the students to recall the memory sentence for this story.

MEMORIZE:

Introduce the poem below, which students can memorize as a way of remembering the key aspects of the story. The text can be recited as poetry, or it can be rapped or sung if the students would like to add melody or beats.

Helios

Great Titan, God of the sun,
A product of heaven and earth, second to no one.
He made sure human beings kept their oaths,
Combining the world and the sky, shining light on both.

The sky god Boreas controlled icy winds and snow,
Arrogant in the strength of the wind he would blow,
He challenged Helios in a competition of power,
But his intentions were nothing but pure and very sour.

They spotted a man on Earth, free of stress,
And attempted to see who could make him undress.
Boreas blew icy cold wind at the man,
Nearly freezing him to death, so he could barely stand.

Helios instead shined warm rays of the sun,
Calming the man so he no longer had to run,
He peacefully took a swim in the lake.
Showing that gentleness beats harshness for kindness's sake!

FOLLOW-UP ACTIVITIES:

1. CREATIVE WRITING:

- Continue to work with the children on their own original poetry based on the story. (Use the word bank created earlier in the week.)

- Have older children work on writing their own version of the story with illustrations. This is best done in their individual notebook, lined on one side and blank on the other. See the Appendix for photos of this kind of notebook with sample student writing and illustrations. Or, record the student's poem in Nyansa's Year One Literature Workbook.

- Close out the story by inviting students to present the poetry, pictures, and/or other writing they have done this week.

2. CLOSING GAME SUGGESTIONS:

- Number Knockout - links and explanations of this game can be found in our Teacher's Guide book, available for purchase on our website.

- Review games - these include Latin and other review games for our literature curriculum. For example, use 3x5 cards. Put the names of the gods and goddesses on one side of the card and what they are known for on a separate 3x5 card. Throughout the weeks, you can review the gods and goddesses by matching the name of the god or goddess with what they are known for. For more ideas, see our Teacher's Guide.

Literature Group Week 16– Helios Day 4

See Learning Through Art

On day four, we encourage you to use the Nyansa Art Curriculum. Students will learn to build observation skills and habits of attention. They will also engage in group discussions that discuss our virtues for the week.

If you do not have the Nyansa Year One Art Curriculum, you can use the illustrations from this week's lessons. Have your students look at the illustration for 2 minutes. After the two minutes, turn over the page. Ask your student to describe the illustration back to you without looking at the picture. Then, discuss how the illustrations for this week tell the story of this week's Greek Myth through the images they observed.

Literature Group Week 17– Hephaestus
Day 1
Lesson 1: Hephaestus - Greek God of Metalworking

Focus Virtue: Honesty is telling the truth.

Focus Vice: Dishonesty is hiding the truth.

Discuss the virtue and what each means. Create a new memory card for each term with its meaning and its opposite on the back of the card. More details can be found in previous weeks. Introduce the story of Artemis by allowing the students two minutes to examine her portrait. Then, turn over the portrait and ask the students to recall what they saw. Use the portrait discussion and the following facts to introduce the story:

Use the following illustrations for this week.

INTRODUCTION:

Hephaestus was the Greek god of metalworking and the forge. Metal working was an important skill in ancient Greece because it enabled them to make useful tools, armor, and weapons, as well as beautiful things like cups, plates, and jewelry. In ancient times, blacksmiths would melt metal in special fireplaces called "forges." They would superheat the fire by blowing on it with a special tool called a bellows. The fire would become so hot it would melt the metal, allowing the smith to bend and shape it. It took years of practice to learn how to control the temperature of the fire, how to hammer the metal evenly, and how to shape the metal. Those who were particularly skilled at metalworking were thought to be blessed by Hephaestus. He was often depicted in Greek art as a cripple or dwarf with a black bushy beard and a large hammer and tongs. His name is closely related to the Greek word for "fire." Like Athena, Hephaestus was thought to give the gifts of skill to mortal men. His sacred animal was the donkey, which you can see him riding in many of his portraits.

READ:

Read the story of Hephaestus (Greek Gods #17). Encourage narration activities as students listen (drawing, writing, etc).

Hephaestus

Hephaestus had a rough start in life. Zeus, the king of heaven, had born Athena all by himself from his powerful brain, and Hera, jealous as always, wanted to have an equally impressive child all by herself. She gave birth to Hephaestus, but when she saw he was ugly and weak, like the flickering flame of a candle, she cast him down to the earth to die. The fall crushed his feet, and he was forever lame. Luckily for Hephaestus, two water goddesses, Eurynome and Thetis, rescued him and raised him. Just like metal is strengthened by being cooled with water, fiery Hephaestus was thrown into the care of the water goddesses, where he grew strong and skilled. Over the years, the god mastered his craft so greatly that he created many beautiful and skillfully wrought items for the gods.

When Hephaestus grew up, he was angry. He should have grown up on Mount Olympus, loved and cared for by Queen Hera herself, but she had thrown him away and pretended she didn't know him. No one on Mount Olympus realized who he was. Only Thetis and Eurynome knew the truth because they had found him, and they had, in turn, told the truth to him. But although the truth made him angry, it did not make Hephaestus hasty. Not at all. Instead, he slowly plotted his revenge. In his giant forge, Hephaestus crafted splendid golden thrones with matching footstools. He sent one to each of the gods on Mount Olympus as a gifts. The gods and goddesses were delighted with the beautifully wrought chairs, and each tried sitting on their gifts. But when Hera sat in her chair, invisible chains sprung up and bound her to the chair. Then, it flipped upside down and hung her helpless in the air. She cried and screamed, but no one could untie her. Eventually, Hera confessed to everyone that she was Hephaestus' mother, and, after some convincing, Hephaestus untied her. From that time on, mother and son worked together, and Hephaestus took his place among the gods on Mount Olympus.

But even after Hera recognized him, Hephaestus never forgot his adoptive mother, Thetis. During the Trojan War, Thetis came to Hephaestus with a special request. Thetis had a beloved son, the splendid Achilles. He was the best soldier in the entire world, but she worried about him because he was mortal. Thetis had bathed him in a special river as a protection, but he still had one weakness - she had held him by his heels, and they were vulnerable! When Thetis heard that her son was going to challenge the brave and glorious Hector in battle, she asked Hephaestus to make him a new set of armor to protect him. Hephaestus loved his adoptive mother, and so he made the most amazing armor ever seen for Achilles. First, he made a shield of layered metal, golden and shining as the sun. It was so bright that mortal men feared to look into it. Hephaestus covered the shield with delicate illustrations of a flowing river, sheep, festivals, fields, and dancing maidens holding hands. The shield strap was made of silver, and Hephaestus also made Achilles a golden helmet and leg guards of shining tin. Achilles wore these splendid gifts during his victorious battle with Hector. Like all mortal men, Achilles was doomed to eventually die, but he did great feats before he died wearing the gifts of Hephaestus.

When Zeus wanted to curse humanity, he asked Hephaestus to craft the first woman, Pandora. Hephaestus fashioned her out of clay and made her a crown of gold. Decorating the crown were hundreds of pictures of plants and animals that he had painstakingly carved. It was so beautiful and delicate, it made Pandora appear even more splendid. Every god gave Pandora a special gift, and then they gave her to the world. (Her name actually means "all gifts!") Humanity thought she was a gift herself, but she was actually the perfect trap. According to Greek myth, Pandora brought pain and sorrow into the world.

In time, Hephaestus married the goddess Aphrodite. As a wedding present, he made his bride the most beautiful chariot. It was made of gold, but the clever god had fashioned it of the thinnest shimmeriest sheets of gold. Normally, golden objects are very heavy, but her chariot was so light it could be pulled by four white doves. The gold gleamed in the sunlight, and the harness was studded with precious gems. Aphrodite loved the chariot, but she did not love Hephaestus. She did not like that Hephaestus was lame, and she sometimes fell in love with better-looking gods instead, which made Hephaestus sad and angry.

Hephaestus also made homes for the gods on Mount Olympus, chariots for his sons, and a jeweled necklace for his daughter. Even more famously, he made armor for the hero Hercules, son of Zeus. Sometimes, his gifts were truly wonderful and precious; other times, they were traps or cursed presents, but they were always beautiful to look at. His immortal life was full of sadness, but his hands were full of beauty and skill.

Language Note: In Latin, Hephaestus is called "Vulcan." We get our word "volcano" from the Greek and Roman God of Fire!

DISCUSS:

Discussion Questions:

1. Were any characters in this story dishonest? What was the consequence of their dishonesty?

2. Would you like Hephaestus to make you a present? Why or why not? Would you trust any present he gave you?

3. Why did Hera throw Hephaestus away? What might have happened if she had loved him instead?

4. Who did love Hephaestus?

5. Have you ever been embarrassed? Were you tempted to lie? What did you do?

MEMORY:

Memory Sentence: Hephaestus was the Greek god of metalworking and the forge.

FOLLOW-UP ACTIVITIES:

1. DRESS UP

- Have the children act out the story. Suggested dress-up items:

crutch (Hephaestus)	tiara (Hera)
hammer	crown (Zeus)
chairs	crown (Pandora)
gold cloth	shield (Achilles)
garland of flowers (Aphrodite)	blue cloak/veil (Thetis)

2. BRAINSTORM

- Use a full-color picture of Hephaestus. Brainstorm words for the people (characters), places (setting), or things (objects) from the story. For more details, see previous lessons.

People
- Hephaestus - weak, small, fiery, clever, abandoned, saved, cherished, grown, angry, vengeful, master craftsman, crafty, gifting, punishing
- Hera - jealous, disappointed, cruel, unkind, abandoning, punished, trapped, tricked
- Zeus - plotting, punishing, tricking, employing, powerful, kingly
- Thetis and Eurynome - rescuing, king, cherishing, rewarded, loved
- Aphrodite - loved, unloving, honored, dishonoring, beautiful, cruel
- Pandora - crafted, beautiful, gifted, deceptive, charming, entrapping
- Achilles - skilled, powerful, loved, protected, blessed

Things
- Hephaestus' forge - hot, fiery, transforming, crafting, smoking
- Golden thrones - beautiful, deceptive, imprisoning, shining
- Pandora's crown - beautiful, intricate, golden, illustrated, ensnaring, treacherous
- Aphrodite's chariot - light, shimmering, bejeweled, magnificent, crafted
- Achilles' armor - golden, shining, powerful, strong, protective, illustrated, prized

Literature Group Week 17– Hephaestus
Day 2

Focus Virtue: Honesty is telling the truth.

Focus Vice: Dishonesty is hiding the truth.

DISCUSS:

- Review the virtue and vice concepts. Have children narrate back the story from the previous day.

- Review the memory sentences presented in the previous session.

FOLLOW-UP ACTIVITIES:

1. DICTATION:

- Individual or in Teams - For more information, see previous weeks.

Pre-K

- Hephaestus - begins with N, R, H, or L
- Pandora - begins with Z, E, O, or P
- Forge- begins with F, R, Q, or I
- Armor - begins with P, K, A, or W

Early Elementary

- Hephaestus was the god of metalworking.

Later Elementary

- Hephaestus was abandoned by Hera at birth. He grew to be an amazing blacksmith. He made the most wonderful things out of metal for the gods and heroes.

2. CREATIVE WRITING:

- Go back to the brainstorming page with the word bank and complete that if there's still more to be done. For more information, see previous lessons.

3. CLOSING GAME SUGGESTIONS:

Number Knockout/ Review Games. See previous lessons for more information.

Literature Group Week 17- Hephaestus Day 3

REVIEW: Review the concepts for the virtues and vices. Use the memory cards created for the previous session. Ask the students to recall the memory sentence for this story.

MEMORIZE:

Introduce the poem below, which students can memorize as a way of remembering the key aspects of the story. The text can be recited as poetry, or it can be rapped or sung if the students would like to add melody or beats.

Hephaestus

Beautifully crafting metal, silver, and gold,
Outcasted by his mother at less than 2 years old
Giving gifts to mortal men named after fire,
Hephaestus created beautiful things that everyone desired.

Hera didn't believe that he could succeed
She treated him like garbage, such an evil deed.
Thetis and Eurynome were water goddesses from Earth
They cared for Hephaestus like mothers since birth.

Hephaestus grew up with anger in his heart,
He was robbed of his mother and from Olympus torn apart.
He trapped Hera in a chair, leaving her helpless,
Forcing her to work with him and become selfless.

He went on to dress the best soldiers in battle,
Hand-crafting lovely chariots, weapons, and saddles.
Adorning his family in the shiniest gold,
The brilliance of Hephaestus would never grow old.

FOLLOW-UP ACTIVITIES:

1. CREATIVE WRITING:

- Continue to work with the children on their own original poetry based on the story. (Use the word bank created earlier in the week.)

- Have older children work on writing their own version of the story with illustrations. This is best done in their individual notebook, lined on one side and blank on the other. See the Appendix for photos of this kind of notebook with sample student writing and illustrations. Or, record the student's poem in Nyansa's Year One Literature Workbook.

- Close out the story by inviting students to present the poetry, pictures, and/or other writing they have done this week.

2. CLOSING GAME SUGGESTIONS:

- Number Knockout - links and explanations of this game can be found in our Teacher's Guide book, available for purchase on our website.

- Review games - these include Latin and other review games for our literature curriculum. For example, use 3x5 cards. Put the names of the gods and goddesses on one side of the card and what they are known for on a separate 3x5 card. Throughout the weeks, you can review the gods and goddesses by matching the name of the god or goddess with what they are known for. For more ideas, see our Teacher's Guide.

Literature Group Week 17– Hephaestus Day 4

See Learning Through Art

On day four, we encourage you to use the Nyansa Art Curriculum. Students will learn to build observation skills and habits of attention. They will also engage in group discussions that discuss our virtues for the week.

If you do not have the Nyansa Year One Art Curriculum, you can use the illustrations from this week's lessons. Have your students look at the illustration for 2 minutes. After the two minutes, turn over the page. Ask your student to describe the illustration back to you without looking at the picture. Then, discuss how the illustrations for this week tell the story of this week's Greek Myth through the images they observed.

Literature Group Week 18 – Hercules
Day 1
Lesson 1: Hercules - Greek Hero

Focus Virtue: Fortitude is staying strong under pressure.

Focus Vice: Faint-heartedness is giving up easily.

Discuss the virtue and what each means. Create a new memory card for each term with its meaning and its opposite on the back of the card. More details can be found in previous weeks. Introduce the story of Artemis by allowing the students two minutes to examine her portrait. Then, turn over the portrait and ask the students to recall what they saw. Use the portrait discussion and the following facts to introduce the story:

Use the following illustrations for this week.

INTRODUCTION:

Of all the virtues, fortitude was one of the ones the Greeks admired the most. They loved that mix of gutsiness and perseverance - that little voice inside that said, "Don't give up! Just keep going! It will be worth it!" Life was difficult, and the Greeks knew very well the rich rewards that perseverance and fortitude often bring. They also loved a good story about a hero working towards an incredible goal and gaining it, even in the face of seemingly impossible pressure.

According to legends, Hercules was the most impressive Greek hero of all time, a man of strength, courage, and most of all, fortitude. Throughout his life, he fought gods and monsters and triumphed every time. But life was not easy for Hercules. He was the son of Zeus and a mortal woman. This made Hera, Zeus' wife, very very jealous. She even tried to kill the infant Hercules when he was born by sending snakes to kill him in his crib. But snakes were no match for Hercules! He grabbed them both and killed them.

READ:

Read the story of Hercules (Greek Gods #18). Encourage narration activities as students listen (drawing, writing, etc).

Hercules

When Hercules was a young man, the goddesses of virtue and vice came to see which of them he would follow. The goddess of vice, Cacia, was plump and covered with jewels. She ran up to Hercules and pulled on his clothes, saying, "Hercules, come, follow me! I will make your way easy. You'll have soft comfy beds to lie on, lots of food to eat, no worry, no pain. Just a happy, easy life. Come! I will show you the way!"

Then the goddess of virtue, Arete, spoke as well, standing farther back. She was dressed in an old, worn robe. She looked thin and tired.

"Hercules," she said, "I will not lie to you. The path I offer to you is hard. It is full of pain and suffering. But, if you follow me, you will do great, noble, amazing things. Everything that is worth doing is hard. If you want friends, you have to be a good friend. If you want the ground to grow food for you, you must care for the ground. If you want to be strong, you must work your body and train it diligently. Every good thing has a cost. But the good things I offer you will last forever, and they are worth fighting and suffering for. Follow me."

Which path do you think Hercules took? That's right! He took the path of virtue. No matter how difficult his job became, Hercules put everything he had into it.

Because Hera hated him so much, she made him go crazy, and while he was crazy, he killed his own sons. Full of horrible sadness, Hercules asked the god Apollo to punish him for his terrible actions. Apollo felt sorry for him, but he told him that he must become the servant of King Eurystheus as a punishment. The king would give Hercules twelve impossible jobs called "The Twelve Labors." If Hercules could accomplish them all, the gods would give him immortality.

Hercules' first "labor" was to kill the Nemean Lion. This horrible beast had been terrorizing the land by snatching every living thing that came its way - sheep, cattle, people - and devouring them! After several days of hunting and tracking, Hercules traced the lion to its den. Hidden beside the mouth of the cave, Hercules watched the lion devour its latest kill, its mane dripping with blood and guts. Silently, he fitted one of his strong arrows to his bow and shot it at the lion. He hit the lion right on its side, but the arrow bounced off! The lion turned, furious, to find his attacker. Seeing Hercules with his bow, the lion bounded forward. Hercules shot another arrow right at the beast's chest. Again, the arrow bounced harmlessly off. In desperation, Hercules raised his club and brought it down on the lion's head just as the lion was jumping to tear out his throat. The impact broke the club in two in Hercules's hand, but for one moment, the lion dropped his head and moaned. Seizing the opportunity, Hercules wrapped his strong arms around the lion's neck, jumped on its back, and braced his legs against the lion's feet. The lion struggled, but Hercules wrapped his arms tighter around the lion's neck. Slowly, the lion fell down dead. Hercules used the lion's own claws to cut the skin off the body. Forever more, he wore that lion skin as his armor to protect him from all weapons.

Several labors later, Eurystheus ordered Hercules to muck the stables of Augeas. In order to accomplish the labor, Hercules would have to clean all the cow poop out of all the stables in just one day. King Augeas had lots and lots and lots of cattle. There were mountains of cow poop - more than a hundred men could move in a week. Augeas didn't think Hercules could accomplish the job, but he thought he might get the stables a little cleaner for nothing, so he offered to pay Hercules if he accomplished the job. The task looked impossible, but Hercules did not despair. Instead, he sat and thought, and then, he knew what to do. All day long, Hercules worked on digging a ditch. He dug a ditch all the way from the stables to the great river Alpheus. Cunningly, Hercules diverted the flow of the river down his ditch. The water wooshed down towards the stables, flooded them, and washed all the cow poop away. The stables were clean but very wet. Augeas was not happy, and he refused to pay Hercules. After Hercules finished his twelve labors, he came back and conquered Augeas as punishment.

Hercules' last labor was to capture Cerberus, Hades' guard dog. This horrible three-headed beast stood at the entrance to hell. He would allow souls to pass him into the shadowy realm of Hades', but if any soul tried to leave, he would tear them to pieces. Cerberus was so fierce that no soul had ever gone deep into Hades' dark realm and returned to tell the tale. But that did not dissuade Hercules. With the favor of fair Persephone, the bride of Hades, he journeyed into the underworld. Persephone agreed to let him attack Cerberus if he promised not to kill him. Hercules agreed. Laying down his weapons, he wrestled the savage beast until he was able to tie him up and lead him out on a leash.

As he emerged from the underworld, dragging Cerberus, he became the first mortal man in Greek myth to conquer death itself. He had completed his twelve labors, and the gods gave him the gift of eternal life. When his natural life ended, the gods took him to Mount Olympus, where he lived forever more. There he married the goddess Hebe and the Greeks worshiped him as a god.

DISCUSS:

Discussion Questions:

1. What did the goddess of vice promise Hercules?
2. What did the goddess of virtue tell Hercules? What did she promise him?
3. What do you think would have happened if Hercules had followed Vice instead? What might his life have looked like?
4. Why did Hercules do the Twelve Labors?
5. According to the myth of Hercules, what did the Greeks think you needed to do to gain the gods' favor?
6. Have you ever felt like something was impossible to do? What did you do? Did you find a way to do it?

MEMORY:

Memory Sentence: Because of his fortitude, Hercules gained immortality.

FOLLOW-UP ACTIVITIES:

1. DRESS UP

- Have the children act out the story. Suggested dress-up items:

bow and arrows	dog leash
crown	garland of flowers (Persephone)
tan blanket (lion)	play jewelry (Cacia)
shovel	old shawl (Arete)

2. BRAINSTORM

- Use a full-color picture of Hercules. Brainstorm words for the people (characters), places (setting), or things (objects) from the story. For more details, see previous lessons.

People
- Hercules - strong, brave, gifted, courageous, persevering, unswerving, imorrtal, divine
- Hera - jealous, murderous, cruel
- Cacia - plump, lazy, deceitful, wicked
- Arete - plain, honest, truthful, virtuous, challenging
- King Eurystheus - demanding, exacting, jealous
- King Augeas - spiteful, mean, miserly, untrustworthy
- Persephone - kind, gracious, beautiful

Things
- Nemean Lion - fierce, prowling, strong, unassailable, defeated
- Cerberus - three-headed, growling, drooling, guarding, beaten
- Augeas' stables - filthy, stinky, gross, washed
- River Alpheus - strong, cool, wet, swift, diverted, cleansing

Places
- Underworld - dark, gloomy, dangerous, deadly
- Mount Olympus - bright, shining, lofty

Literature Group Week 18- Hercules
Day 2

Focus Virtue: Fortitude is staying strong under pressure.

Focus Vice: Faint-heartedness is giving up easily.

DISCUSS:

- Review the virtue and vice concepts. Have children narrate back the story from the previous day.
- Review the memory sentences presented in the previous session.

FOLLOW-UP ACTIVITIES:

1. DICTATION:

- Individual or in Teams - For more information, see previous weeks.

Pre-K

- Hercules - begins with B, N, H, or P.
- Labors - begins with L, H, K, or R
- Stables - begins with R, L, D, or S
- Olympus - begins with E, T, C, or O

Early Elementary

- Hercules completed twelve labors.

Later Elementary

- Hera hated Hercules. She made his life difficult. Hercules completed twelve labors. The gods gave him immortality.

2. CREATIVE WRITING:

- Go back to the brainstorming page with the word bank and complete that if there's still more to be done. For more information, see previous lessons.

3. CLOSING GAME SUGGESTIONS:

Number Knockout/ Review Games. See previous lessons for more information.

Literature Group Week 18- Hercules
Day 3

Focus Virtue: Fortitude is staying strong under pressure.

Focus Vice: Faint-heartedness is giving up easily.

No poem for this week's lesson.

FOLLOW-UP ACTIVITIES:

1. CREATIVE WRITING:

- Continue to work with the children on their own original poetry based on the story. (Use the word bank created earlier in the week.)

- Have older children work on writing their own version of the story with illustrations. This is best done in their individual notebook, lined on one side and blank on the other. See the Appendix for photos of this kind of notebook with sample student writing and illustrations. Or, record the student's poem in Nyansa's Year One Literature Workbook.

- Close out the story by inviting students to present the poetry, pictures, and/or other writing they have done this week.

2. CLOSING GAME SUGGESTIONS:

- Number Knockout - links and explanations of this game can be found in our Teacher's Guide book, available for purchase on our website.

- Review games - these include Latin and other review games for our literature curriculum. For example, use 3x5 cards. Put the names of the gods and goddesses on one side of the card and what they are known for on a separate 3x5 card. Throughout the weeks, you can review the gods and goddesses by matching the name of the god or goddess with what they are known for. For more ideas, see our Teacher's Guide.

Literature Group Week 18- Hercules
Day 4

See Learning Through Art

See previous weeks for more instructions.

Literature Group Week 19 – Medusa
Day 1
Lesson 1: Medusa - Greek Monster

Focus Virtue: Courage is doing the right thing even when it's scary.

Focus Vice: Cowardice is letting fear control your actions.

Discuss the virtue and what each means. Create a new memory card for each term with its meaning and its opposite on the back of the card. More details can be found in previous weeks. Introduce the story of Artemis by allowing the students two minutes to examine her portrait. Then, turn over the portrait and ask the students to recall what they saw. Use the portrait discussion and the following facts to introduce the story:

Use the following illustrations for this week.

INTRODUCTION:

Every culture has its own monsters, and the Greeks had some spectacularly scary ones. From the sphinx with her riddles to the bull-headed minotaur in the deep dark caves, Greek stories were full of monsters. One of the creepiest monsters was Medusa. She was one of three sisters - the Gorgons. They lived on the Island of Cisthene off the coast of modern-day Turkey.

The sisters were extremely ugly, with huge boar tusks, large tongues hanging out of their mouths, scruffy beards, and golden wings curled batlike over their backs. Medusa was not as ugly as her sisters, but each wavy lock of her long hair was a hissing venomous snake. She was so terrifying to behold that one look at her face would turn a person into stone! All the warriors feared to fight her, for how could you defeat a monster you could not even look at?

Read the story of Medusa (Greek Monster #19). Encourage narration activities as students listen (drawing, writing, etc).

Medusa

Perseus was one of the Greek's greatest heroes. His mother was the beautiful princess Danae, and his father was Zeus almighty. Over his glorious lifetime, he fought monsters, saved princesses, won competitions, braved the ocean, and gained a kingdom.

When Perseus was a young man, one of the local kings, King Polydektes, asked Perseus to bring him the head of Medusa. (The king was hoping Perseus would die and he would be able to marry Perseus' mother.) Perseus had offered to bring the king whatever he wanted, and so he could not say no. No man had ever dared to fight the Gorgons and lived to tell the tale, but there is always a first.

As he journeyed towards the Island of Cisthene, Perseus began to pray. He had no idea how to kill Medusa, and so he offered up his prayers to Athena, the helper of the bold and brave. Bright-eyed Athena appeared before him in full armor.

"Looking for Medusa, are you, my fine hero?" asked Athena with a smile.

"Yes, oh gracious goddess. Would you show me the way?" replied Perseus.

"I could," replied Athena, "but you would never defeat Medusa as you are. To fight Medusa, you will need Hades' invisibility helmet, the sword of Hephaestus, and the winged sandals of Hermes."

"How am I to find those things?" asked Perseus.

"The nymphs have them, but even I do not know the whereabouts of the nymphs. To find them, you must get the Graeae hags to tell you. I will lead you to them." And she led him to the Island of Cisthene, where the Graeae lived, keeping guard over their sisters, the Gorgons.

Now the Graeae were three ugly old hags made from the foam of the sea. They were so old and so frail that they had only one eye and one tooth between them, which they took turns sharing. A foul smell wafted from them, and their faces were as horrible as death. Silently, Perseus snuck up to them. One began to pass the eye and tooth to her sister, and quick as a flash, he grabbed them and jumped away.

"Who is there? What have you done!?" hissed the Graeae, feeling around with their hands for the thief.

"It is I, Perseus," he replied, stepping back, "and I need your help."

"We don't help mortal boys. Be gone!" they growled.

"Then I will take your eye and your tooth with me!" said Perseus, and he began to stomp away.

"WAIT." said the oldest Graeae, "What do you need?" Perseus explained. The three hags put their heads together. After whispering for a bit, they agreed to show him to the nymphs. Upon the highest cliff on Cisthene, the hags stopped, and the nymphs appeared. Perseus returned the eye and tooth, and the Graeae hobbled away. The nymphs were impressed to see that the Graeae had aided Perseus, so when they heard what Perseus wanted, they were happy to lend him the magical items. With grave reverence, Perseus put Hephaestus' sword in his belt. Made of adamantium, it glittered like diamonds, and its edge was sharp enough to cut iron. Then, he strapped Hermes' winged sandals onto his feet. Finally, he strapped Hades' helmet of invisibility onto his head, and he disappeared to all earthly eyes. Athena, of course, could still see him, and she led him to the cave of the Gorgons.

A horrible smell was wafting out of the cave as if it were full of dead things. Perseus felt his stomach turn.

"Remember," said Athena, "do not look straight at Medusa, or you will turn to stone. Look only at your shield!" Perseus promised to do as she said, and he scrambled down the rocks into the cave. Just inside the cave were several stone statues - Medusa's victims. His heart was pounding, but he kept moving on.

He hadn't gone far when he heard a great hissing sound, as if a thousand snakes were slithering through the cave. Quickly, he turned his shield so he could see the cave reflected on its bright surface. Staring only at the shield, Perseus shuffled on, being careful not to allow his eyes to move away from it. He came to a bend in the cave. Cautiously, he turned his shield so it would reflect the space beyond the bend. Perseus peered into the shield to see. There, lying on the ground around the bend, was Medusa sleeping. Her wings were furled behind her, and thousands of entwined snakes encircled her head, hissing softly. Even reflected, she was so horrible to see that he almost fainted. But gathering his courage, he pulled Hephaestus' sword from his belt and slowly tiptoed around the corner. Watching his reflection in the shield, he raised his sword, and with one horrible slash, he cut off Medusa's head! She gave one earth-splitting scream, and then the hissing stopped. Without looking down, Perseus bent and grabbed a handful of her snake hair. He lifted her head and put it into a silver bag, which he strung onto his back. Just then, he heard the sounds of screaming and scraping. Medusa's sisters had heard her die and were coming to kill him. Perseus flew into the air on Herme's sandals. Cloaked with Hades' helmet, the Gorgons could not even see him. They ran right past him, and he was free!

Perseus realized that Medusa's head was dangerous, even though she was dead, and so he gave it to Athena. Proud of her warrior, Athena strapped Medusa's head to the front of her shield. From then on, whoever looked at Athena's shield died of fright. Perseus returned his borrowed gifts to the nymphs, and the favor of the gods went with him wherever he went.

DISCUSS:

Discussion Questions:

1. What did the goddess of vice promise Hercules?
2. What did the goddess of virtue tell Hercules? What did she promise him?
3. What do you think would have happened if Hercules had followed Vice instead? What might his life have looked like?
4. Why did Hercules do the Twelve Labors?
5. According to the myth of Hercules, what did the Greeks think you needed to do to gain the gods' favor?
6. Have you ever felt like something was impossible to do? What did you do? Did you find a way to do it?

MEMORY:

Memory Sentence: Brave Perseus killed Medusa.

FOLLOW-UP ACTIVITIES:

1. DRESS UP

- Have the children act out the story. Suggested dress-up items:

aluminum helmet	tin shield
sandals with paper wings	flower garlands (nymphs)
play sword	fake snake hair twisties/foam
golf balls (eye of Graeae	

2. BRAINSTORM

- Use a full-color picture of Medusa. Brainstorm words for the people (characters), places (setting), or things (objects) from the story. For more details, see previous lessons.

People
- Perseus - brave courageous, humble, intelligent, clever, bold, daring
- Athena - wise helpful, guiding, stately, beautiful, goddess
- Medusa - terrifying, scaly, horrible, frightening, destroyed
- Graeae - old, gray, toothless, blind, coerced, guiding
- Nymphs - impressed, honoring, gifted, hidden, found
- King Polydektes - evil, selfish, plotting

Things
- Hades' helmet - borrowed, aiding
- Hermes' sandals - swift, winged, borrowed
- Perseus' shield - shiny, reflective
- Athena's shield - adorned, improved

Places
- Island of Cisthene - scary, haunted

Literature Group Week 19– Medusa
Day 2

Focus Virtue: Courage is doing the right thing even when it's scary.

Focus Vice: Cowardice is letting fear control your actions.

DISCUSS:

- Review the virtue and vice concepts. Have children narrate back the story from the previous day.
- Review the memory sentences presented in the previous session.

FOLLOW-UP ACTIVITIES:

1. DICTATION:

- Individual or in Teams - For more information, see previous weeks.

Pre-K

- Medusa - begins with M, C, H, or L
- Perseus - begins with T, O, P or U
- Gorgon- begins with B, G, Q, or I
- Athena - begins with P, K, E, or A

Early Elementary

- Perseus destroyed the monster Medusa.

Later Elementary

- Perseus set out to kill the monster Medusa. Athena helped him get special tools. By watching the reflections in his shield, Perseus was able to destroy Medusa.

2. CREATIVE WRITING:

- Go back to the brainstorming page with the word bank and complete that if there's still more to be done. For more information, see previous lessons.

3. CLOSING GAME SUGGESTIONS:

Number Knockout/ Review Games. See previous lessons for more information.

Literature Group Week 19– Medusa
Day 3

REVIEW: Review the concepts for the virtues and vices. Use the memory cards created for the previous session. Ask the students to recall the memory sentence for this story.

MEMORIZE:

Introduce the poem below, which students can memorize as a way of remembering the key aspects of the story. The text can be recited as poetry, or it can be rapped or sung if the students would like to add melody or beats.

Medusa

Statues in place of the lives she takes,
Long hair flowing with venomous snakes,
Glancing at her enemies to turn them to stone,
Medusa, the monster, had no mercy to be shown.

In order for the local king to be wed,
He had to have Medusa's head.
So he sent Perseus on a quest to defeat her,
His instructions were given in a careless blur.

Luckily, Athena had the warrior recipes,
And gave Perseus the tools of war and necessities.
Armed with invisibility, wings, and a sword,
For his bravery, he should have gotten an award.

Finally, he faced Medusa in a deep, dark cave,
And cut off her head with his sword and a wave.
Given to Athena was her head still filled with power,
Perseus lived on with godly favor every hour.

FOLLOW-UP ACTIVITIES:

1. CREATIVE WRITING:

- Continue to work with the children on their own original poetry based on the story. (Use the word bank created earlier in the week.)

- Have older children work on writing their own version of the story with illustrations. This is best done in their individual notebook, lined on one side and blank on the other. See the Appendix for photos of this kind of notebook with sample student writing and illustrations. Or, record the student's poem in Nyansa's Year One Literature Workbook.

- Close out the story by inviting students to present the poetry, pictures, and/or other writing they have done this week.

2. CLOSING GAME SUGGESTIONS:

- Number Knockout - links and explanations of this game can be found in our Teacher's Guide book, available for purchase on our website.

- Review games - these include Latin and other review games for our literature curriculum. For example, use 3x5 cards. Put the names of the gods and goddesses on one side of the card and what they are known for on a separate 3x5 card. Throughout the weeks, you can review the gods and goddesses by matching the name of the god or goddess with what they are known for. For more ideas, see our Teacher's Guide.

Literature Group Week 19– Medusa Day 4

See Learning Through Art

On day four, we encourage you to use the Nyansa Art Curriculum. Students will learn to build observation skills and habits of attention. They will also engage in group discussions that discuss our virtues for the week.

If you do not have the Nyansa Year One Art Curriculum, you can use the illustrations from this week's lessons. Have your students look at the illustration for 2 minutes. After the two minutes, turn over the page. Ask your student to describe the illustration back to you without looking at the picture. Then, discuss how the illustrations for this week tell the story of this week's Greek Myth through the images they observed.

Literature Group Week 20– Pan
Day 1
Lesson 1: Pan - Greek God of the Mountains, Flocks, Joy, Fear

Focus Virtue: Joy is enthusiastically enjoying your blessings.

Focus Vice: Despair is giving up hope when things get hard.

Discuss the virtue and what each means. Create a new memory card for each term with its meaning and its opposite on the back of the card. More details can be found in previous weeks. Introduce the story of Artemis by allowing the students two minutes to examine her portrait. Then, turn over the portrait and ask the students to recall what they saw. Use the portrait discussion and the following facts to introduce the story:
Use the following illustrations for this week.

INTRODUCTION:

Have you ever done something that was really, really fun but also scary? Maybe you sang in the school play or took a dive off the high diving board into a pool. Maybe you splashed in the crashing waves of the ocean or rode on the back of a motorcycle. Do you know that thrilling feeling - that excitement that creates a pit in your stomach? Well, the Greeks had a god for that, and his name was Pan. He was the god of mountains, shepherds, flocks, joy, and fear. From the chest up, Pan looked like a very hairy man with a snub nose, pointy ears, dark curly hair, a beard, and small horns coming out of his head. From the waist down, he looked like a goat with hairy legs and slender little hooves! The Romans called him "Faunus," which is where we get the word "faun" - a mythic creature, half-man, and half-goat, that you may have met in some fantasy books. Pan lived high in the mountains among the sheep. He loved to sing and dance and play his musical pipes under the sun while he chased the wild nymphs. The Greeks believed he was mischievous and full of laughter and joy. In art, they often drew him with dancing goat legs and his own beloved pan-pipes, called a "syrinx."

READ:

Read the story of Pan (Greek God #20). Encourage narration activities as students listen (drawing, writing, etc).

Pan

Pan was the son of the god Hermes. The messenger god had fallen in love with a beautiful girl named Penelope who lived in the mountains. She had long black curly hair which fell almost to her feet. Hermes loved her so much that he pretended to be a shepherd so that he could walk in the mountains, hoping for a glimpse of her. Eventually, Hermes married Penelope, and they lived together in a house high in the mountains among the sweet clover and the gentle noises of sheep.

Penelope was delighted when she realized she was going to have a baby. How wonderful it would be to be a mother! She imagined holding a soft, little snuggly baby, all sweet and perfect. When the time came for her to give birth, she summoned a nurse to help her deliver the baby. She gave birth, but the baby looked very strange. When the nurse saw the child, she screamed and ran out of the room, out of the house, and down the mountain, as fast as her legs could carry her. Penelope was startled! Why had the nurse been frightened? She looked down and panicked. Her baby had a beard! And horns! And goat legs!

When he saw the nurse run out screaming, Hermes ran in. He had been waiting anxiously outside to see his child, but now something seemed wrong. His wife was crying, the nurse was gone, and the baby was lying on the bed. Walking over, he picked up the hairy child. Pan looked up at his father with a twinkle in his little eyes. Pan's hairy face crinkled up in a laugh, and he kicked his little goat legs happily. Hermes looked into the face of his son for a moment, and then he too began to laugh. Together, they laughed and laughed and laughed. What a merry little creature, thought Hermes. He hugged his little son - he was perfect. Gently, he wrapped the boy in the soft skins of mountain rabbits and tucked him in the crook of his arm.

Hermes was so proud of his little boy that he took him away and brought him to Mount Olympus. Holding him up, Hermes showed him off to Aphrodite, Athena, Apollo, and all the immortal gods. One by one, they came to look at the new immortal child, and one by one, they each began to laugh. His face was so funny and strange, and he filled their hearts with joy and wonder. Soon, the shining halls of Mount Olympus echoed with laughter and merriment. Almighty Zeus heard the noise and came striding in, curious to see the reason behind all the celebration. Looking down at the snub nose and hairy little face, Zeus loved his grandson, and his grim face broke into a smile. They decided to call him "Pan," which means "all," because he filled all of their hearts with joy.

Pan grew up in the mountains among the nymphs. In all the stories, they say he was a wild god, full of mischief and mirth. Once, he fell in love with a nymph named Echo, and he chased her for many months through the mountains. At first, she did not love him. In fact, the other nymphs captured Pan and shaved off his beard to punish him for annoying her so much. But eventually, Pan won Echo's heart. He would teach her songs, and she would sing them back. The hills rang with the notes of his pipes and the sound of her singing back to him. So if you ever hear an echo in the mountains, think of Pan and his mountain bride, singing back and forth to each other among the majestic hills.

Language Note: *Pan's name means "all" in Greek, and we get our English word "panic" from his name. Panic is a sudden feeling of fear.*

DISCUSS:

Discussion Questions:

1. Who demonstrated joy in this story?
2. Why did the nurse run away when she saw Pan? How do you think she was feeling?
3. What did Hermes think of Pan? Why do you think his reaction was different than the nurse's and Penelope's?
4. What fills you with joy? Is that joy ever mixed with fear? Is there anything you like to do that makes you a little afraid, but you love it anyways?

MEMORY:

Memory Sentence: Pan brought joy to all the gods.

FOLLOW-UP ACTIVITIES:

1. DRESS UP

- Have the children act out the story. Suggested dress-up items:

hat with wings (Hermes)	baby blanket
dress (Penelope)	crown (Zeus)
doctor kit (nurse)	pan pipes (Pan)
baby doll (Pan)	

2. BRAINSTORM

- Use a full-color picture of Medusa. Brainstorm words for the people (characters), places (setting), or things (objects) from the story. For more details, see previous lessons.

People
- Hermes - loving, happy, excited, worried, thrilled, laughing, amused, overjoyed, caring, quick, proud
- Penelope - beautiful, hopeful, excited, disappointed, frightened
- Nurse - helpful, caring, frightened, dismayed
- Pan - ugly, hairy, strange, frightening, amusing, funny, merry, laughing, beloved, wild, horned, hooved
- Echo - loved, swift, musical, beautiful, nymph
- Gods - loving, amused, laughing, joyful

Things
- Syrinx - musical, bright, eerie, echoing

Places
- Mountain - green, high, windy, majestic, lofty, grassy
- Mount Olympus - lofty, shining, bright

Literature Group Week 20- Pan
Day 2

Focus Virtue: Joy is enthusiastically enjoying your blessings.

Focus Vice: Despair is giving up hope when things get hard.

DISCUSS:

- Review the virtue and vice concepts. Have children narrate back the story from the previous day.
- Review the memory sentences presented in the previous session.

FOLLOW-UP ACTIVITIES:

1. DICTATION:

- Individual or in Teams - For more information, see previous weeks.

Pre-K

- Pan- begins with P, Q, A, or U
- Hermes- begins with I, O, P, or H
- Nymph - begins with H, N, R, or T
- Faun - begins with B, F, S, or C

Early Elementary

- Baby Pan brought joy to all the gods.

Later Elementary

- Pan was born with a beard, horns, and goat legs! He scared his nurse, but the gods thought he was very funny.

2. CREATIVE WRITING:

- Go back to the brainstorming page with the word bank and complete that if there's still more to be done. For more information, see previous lessons.

3. CLOSING GAME SUGGESTIONS:

Number Knockout/ Review Games. See previous lessons for more information.

Literature Group Week 20– Pan
Day 3

REVIEW: Review the concepts for the virtues and vices. Use the memory cards created for the previous session. Ask the students to recall the memory sentence for this story.

MEMORIZE:

Introduce the poem below, which students can memorize as a way of remembering the key aspects of the story. The text can be recited as poetry, or it can be rapped or sung if the students would like to add melody or beats.

Medusa

Greek god of the mountains, controlling joy and fear,
Capable of producing laughter or tears,
Hairy and stout, half goat, half man,
The mischievous creature held the name Pan.

His father was Hermes, his mother Penelope of the mountains,
The couple moved peacefully among the slopes and fountains.
When Penelope gave birth, the nurse was filled with fright,
She screamed and ran away with all her might!

The baby born was no normal babe at all,
He had hairy feet, a beard, and goat legs far too tall!
But Hermes loved him and was filled with joy.
He hurried to the gods to present his new baby boy.

Zeus, too, fell in love with his unique grandson,
He set him free to live amongst the nymphs and run.
Pan soon fell in love with Echo, winning her heart.
In the mountains, they lived, and were never apart.

FOLLOW-UP ACTIVITIES:

1. CREATIVE WRITING:

- Continue to work with the children on their own original poetry based on the story. (Use the word bank created earlier in the week.)

- Have older children work on writing their own version of the story with illustrations. This is best done in their individual notebook, lined on one side and blank on the other. See the Appendix for photos of this kind of notebook with sample student writing and illustrations. Or, record the student's poem in Nyansa's Year One Literature Workbook.

- Close out the story by inviting students to present the poetry, pictures, and/or other writing they have done this week.

2. CLOSING GAME SUGGESTIONS:

- Number Knockout - links and explanations of this game can be found in our Teacher's Guide book available for purchase on our website.

- Review games - these include Latin and other review games for our literature curriculum. For example, use 3x5 cards. Put the names of the gods and goddesses on one side of the card and what they are known for on a separate 3x5 card. Throughout the weeks, you can review the gods and goddesses by matching the name of the god or goddess with what they are known for. For more ideas, see our Teacher's Guide.

Literature Group Week 20– Pan
Day 4

See Learning Through Art

On day four, we encourage you to use the Nyansa Art Curriculum. Students will learn to build observation skills and habits of attention. They will also engage in group discussions that discuss our virtues for the week.

If you do not have the Nyansa Year One Art Curriculum, you can use the illustrations from this week's lessons. Have your students look at the illustration for 2 minutes. After the two minutes, turn over the page. Ask your student to describe the illustration back to you without looking at the picture. Then, discuss how the illustrations for this week tell the story of this week's Greek Myth through the images they observed.

www.ingramcontent.com/pod-product-compliance
Lightning Source LLC
Chambersburg PA
CBHW080957120626
46546CB00010B/2937